ADVENT

ADVENT

by

JEAN DANIÉLOU

Translated by Rosemary Sheed

SHEED AND WARD

NEW YORK • 1951

NIHIL OBSTAT: EDUARDUS MAHONEY, S.T.D.
CENSOR DEPUTATUS

IMPRIMATUR E. MORROGH BERNARD
VIC. GEN.

WESTMONASTERII, DIE 27A JULII, 1950

CONTENTS

INTRODUCTION

—

To ENGAGE in missionary work is at once to be faced with the problem of the relationship between Catholicism and the non-Christian religions. Along more general lines, it is a question that is engrossing everyone today. What is there in Christianity that transcends the other religions? That is one of the objections most often put by those around us and it finds us too often defenceless. You yourselves agree, they say to us, that in Buddhism, for instance, there is profound wisdom; that there is a deep and strong spirit of religion in Islam. Then why not allow that there are a certain number of religions in the world, which we will not say are all equally valuable, but which all suit different temperaments, races or countries? After all, you agree that men of good will can be saved, even outside the Christian framework, in non-Christian religions. What, then, can this transcendence of Christianity mean?

The same question appears on a more practical level in the missionary field. There are two possible views for the missionary to take of non-Christian civilisations and religions, and it is often hard for him to see which is the truer. On the one hand there is the favourable, optimistic view, which sees all the good in them, all that seems a preparation for Christianity, all that would become perfect if carried a little further and crowned with Christian ideals. But on the other hand, missionaries also realise only too well that these religions are themselves the greatest obstacle to Christianity, and that if a Mussulman, for instance, is to be converted he must renounce what constitutes his faith in all in which that faith goes against Christian belief. Kraemer's book[1] is interesting in that it brings this opposition into relief by pushing the pessimistic attitude as far as it will go: you must realise that the Gospel is an absolute paradox, a complete reversal of the values held by non-Christian religions and civilisations; any attempts to adapt will only end in confusion; you must simply announce the Gospel as it stands, and trust Christ's strength and grace to get it accepted.

This problem forces us to reflect rather more deeply upon the exact relationship between these non-Christian religions and Christianity. Is it total opposition, as between error and truth, so that we see the world as a conflict between Catholicism and non-Christian religions? Or do we, on the contrary, see Christianity as completing and perfecting what is found in a more rudimentary state in the other religions? And, if we consider Christianity a fulfilment of what is in the other religions, where is its transcendence, and how does it represent something higher than they? These are the two positions between which missionary thought is often seen to hesitate.

I should like to show that we come upon this same opposition in other domains. It strikes us first in the attitude taken by the Fathers of the Church and the first Christians towards the pagan religions around them, and towards Judaism. But we find its origins in the very heart of Scripture and the Old Testament. In fact, the relation of Christianity to other religions is in part historical —that is to say, there is a "chronological" relationship

[1] *Le message chrétien dans un monde non-chrétien.*

between Christianity and the other religions insofar as
it represents the end and fulfilment of all the rest; but
it is at the same time a dramatic relationship—that is to
say, that if it is true that Christianity fulfils, it is also true
that it destroys, so that, on the one hand, pagan religions
find their flowering in it, yet on the other they die to give
it place. It is only by thus uniting these two aspects that
we can see all that is involved in the problem of evangelising different civilisations.

It is most striking to see that the first Christians found
themselves in exactly the same position with regard to the
world around them as our missionaries are in pagan lands
today: they, too, were a small minority bringing into a
completely closed and hostile world a message quite
foreign to it. Saint Paul, going to Athens for the first time
and preaching the Gospel on the Areopagus, was in
exactly the same situation as the first missionaries who
went to China or Japan and preached to the sages there.

What was the attitude of these first Christians to the
pagan religions surrounding them? Surprisingly enough,
a certain number felt the same profound optimism that
various of our contemporaries feel towards the oriental
religions. I am thinking particularly of two writers of the
second century, Justin Martyr and Clement of Alexandria.
Both men had the idea that in pagan philosophies there
was some sort of presence of the Word, of the Logos, some
sort of divine light that enlightened men and gave them
whatever of truth was in them. It followed, then, that a
Plato, for example, or a Socrates, could not have seen the
truth he did without some sort of illumination. Therefore
the Word, who was to communicate Himself in His
fulness in Christian Revelation, was already in some way
present.

What was true of the pagan civilisations was of course even truer of Judaism. If the Word was in some way present in them, how much more was God acting upon the Jewish people, assuring them a part of the truth! I am emphasising this, because this very thing was then being contested by some who saw an absolute and radical opposition between Christianity and Judaism. Marcion in the second century developed this antithesis to its furthest point. He took from the Old Testament all the more crudely and scandalously anthropomorphic expressions about God, all the passages dealing with God's jealousy, God's vengeance, God's hatred for this people or that, to show how different was the Old Testament God of justice and rigour from the New Testament God of love, how opposed the particularist God of the Old Testament, who took interest in only one people and hated the others, to the universalist God, Father of men, of the New Testament. He thought by this to prove that there was a total opposition between Christianity and Judaism, that they were the work of different gods, and that the efforts made by early Christians to show that the doctrines were related were illusory and vain: they must accept the fact that Christianity was a complete novelty—that is to say, that nothing that came before was in any way connected with it; before, everything was evil, it was an unhappy world, governed by a malevolent god; with Christ we entered on a new era in a world of love and mercy. And obviously he saw this opposition as even stronger in regard to the pagan religions.

With this radical notion before them, the Fathers of the Church were obliged to try and define the principle governing the relation between Christianity and what had come before. They found this principle in the conception of a progressive plan of God. As Saint Irenaeus saw it, God's plan had always been the same—that is to say, that God never had any design other than *instaurare omnia in Christo*. Man is, to start with, a carnal being to whom divine things are quite foreign, and who would be blinded if he saw too great a glory. God had to adapt Himself to man's weakness, to treat him as a small child to whom one can at first say only simple things. Thou shalt not kill, thou shalt not steal, honour thy father and thy mother. Those are very simple things, and we find them also in pagan religions, for instance in the wisdom of China. Thus, bit by bit, by a sort of education, a sort of pedagogy—I am using a word Saint Paul used first when he said "the Law was our pedagogue in Christ" (Gal. iii. 24), which the Fathers never wearied of quoting—God led mankind on till it was able to bear full divine revelation, till it was in some degree ripe for Christ; so that, as Scripture says, Christ came in the fulness of times. There was need for this sort of preparation, and for Christ to come only when it reached its climax.

In this perspective you see quite well how there can be a continuity—and there is, indeed, a real continuity—between Judaism and Christianity, between the pagan civilisations and Christianity, in this sense, that they all fit into the same design, that they are the work of the same God. That is why Marcion was wrong when he said they were two worlds quite cut off from each other. It was the same Word who was secretly at work in the non-Christian world and in the Jewish world, and who, having taught man to know His way, then adapted Himself to man's way. It was necessary—according to Saint Irenaeus' most beautiful line of thought—for man to take on divine habits, and God to take on human' because the Incarnation itself was not something thought up in a hurry, and every part of God's work upon us takes place in time. The same is true of the development of our souls; the history of mankind itself is reproduced in them, and we find they also need to be habituated gradually to divine things.

There is, at the same time, a break in continuity—that is to say that between the time when Christ was given to us and the time when He was only being announced and prepared for, there is an abyss. And that is what really makes the essential difference between Christianity and either Judaism or the non-Christian religions. The Fathers did not at first think this difference had any bearing on actual doctrine: the Jews had already a great part of our Revelation. And, as they thought, several of the pagan philosophers had already a certain knowledge of God; even Saint Augustine tells us that, to him, it seemed that Plato had known the mystery of the Blessed Trinity. The gulf between the Old and New Testaments is the gulf between the promise of a thing and the reality of that thing. And this brings us back to the fact that Christianity is essentially a *life*, and not essentially a philosophy. For us, to be Christian is to live divinely, that is, to have grace within us and to have intimacy with God. And this was something *utterly new*.

In one very fine passage Saint Irenaeus writes: "You must realise that He who was promised has brought something totally new, by giving us Himself. When a king is coming he sends envoys to his servants, so that they may make ready to receive him; but when the king actually arrives, and they have the joy that was promised them, and taste the freedom he brings them, and share his vision and hear his words and enjoy his gifts—what man in his senses would ask if there was any difference between this and his former state of expectation?" This shows us that to a man such as Irenaeus there was a very palpable discontinuity, something fundamentally new in Christianity, and yet this fundamental newness did not prevent it from fitting into a continuity and unity with all that had gone before.

The first aspect, then, of the thought of the Church Fathers is this optimism by which they could show Christianity as a continuation and completion of the other religions. Beside this, they have another view which appears exactly to contradict it, which stresses the other, the dramatic aspect of the question. In this view Christianity is no longer considered as the development of a plan carried out with a sort of infallible certitude, by which God bit by bit completes the work of unifying all things in Christ, but as a struggle between Christ and the forces of evil, a struggle in which mankind is at once the player and the stake.

We find first in the Gospel, and then in the thought of the Fathers, this vision of a struggle in which Christ battles with those mysterious powers in the background of human existence which represent a world of beings unfaithful to God and hostile to man; man is their prey and victim so that—and this is most important in the thought of the Fathers—he is not so much the culprit as the victim; the prey of evil forces whom Christ came primarily to set free, rather than a sinner who must make expiation. The notion of expiation was there, too, but it was secondary. Above all, they had in a very high degree a sense of the horror of the state mankind had got into, and from which Christ had come to set us free.

From this point of view the non-Christian religions

immediately appear in a quite different light, not as preparations and stages on the road towards Christianity, but forces fighting against it; the relation between them and Christianity will now seem not to be a continuity at all but a conflict. And in this connection we may recall all those texts where the Fathers of the Church tell us that the essential part of Baptism for a pagan is the renunciation of the works and pomps of Satan—another way of saying idolatry, that is, pagan religion. For it was in fact regarded as an actual worship of Satan, which converts had to renounce to become Christians.

How, then, could the Fathers of the Church manage to reconcile the two positions? By making a distinction—and we do the same today—between the two elements in the non-Christian world, that is to say, by recognising that there were at once real *values*, as a Justin, a Clement or a Saint Augustine did with Greek philosophy and with Plato, and *acts*—idolatrous worship and magical practices which were literally diabolic—by which mankind was bound to the forces fighting against God. Thence came the necessary ambiguity of the position. It is interesting to see that these two currents were at the very root of Christianity from the beginning, and that this antinomy which we keep coming up against today was fully in evidence even then.

That this is so is because this opposition is part of the very make-up of Christian revelation, and one of the essential aspects of the Bible. There is one notion of capital importance in the Bible—the absolute centre of all its meaning—which all too often we do not understand: the idea of *covenant*. The word is not well chosen: it is a translation of the Hebrew *berith*, which means pact or engagement; the Greek translates it either as *diatheke*—an arrangement made by one party in favour of another—or *syntheke*—a bilateral contract. I am stating this so precisely because these ideas will be important in what I have to say later. The Latin, in its turn, translates it either by *foedus*—a bilateral treaty—or by *testamentum*. This brings us to the word Testament, which is the one we use in speaking of the Old and the New Testament, which means, in fact, the Old and the New Covenant.

What was this covenant, this testament? It was God's promise to Abraham of three things: first to lead his people into the Promised Land, the land of Chanaan; second, that of his race He should be born who would save the world; and lastly, that all the nations of the earth should be blessed in his seed. But note that this was not the first covenant to be made. We have in the Bible one passage which is extremely curious for the light it throws on the whole thought of Scripture, the story of the Flood. In this story we see God after the Flood telling Noe that henceforward He would make a covenant with him not to upset the natural order of things again, and that the sign of this promise was to be the rainbow: for whenever God saw it He would remember His covenant and stop the rain.

Whenever, later, the Jews wanted to remind God of His covenant, that is, of the promises He had made them, they always began with this: "Thou, who by thy faithfulness, maintainest the order of the world, and who art therefore faithful to the promise thou hast made to Noe, be faithful also to the promise thou hast made to thy people, to the promise thou hast made to Abraham." This meant that, just as God is faithful in the natural order—this was the Jewish idea: if the sun rose every day, it was not because of some physical determinism, but because of God's faithfulness, for there was nothing impersonal about creation—so in the same way—and this is the more important thing—God is faithful to the plan He has made in the order of grace: nothing will stop its being carried out, and nothing will ever change it.

Man can do nothing to stop the plan. Human freedom has no part here, for the plan is carried out independently of man's fidelity. Had it been a contract between ourselves and God—which, you remember, some of the words given for it suggest—and if, therefore, one contracting party could be freed from his obligations insofar as the other did not fulfil his, then the alliance would have been broken long ago. Since man has not carried out his obligations, God would not have been bound by His word. Now, Saint Paul tells us, what it is most important for us to realise is that what joins us to God is not a bilateral contract, as the Pharisees thought, but a unilateral promise. God's promise, that is to say, is not at the mercy of our infidelities; it is at the mercy of our infidelities insofar as our infidelities prevent us from getting the fruits of the promise, but not insofar as the promise could ever be revoked. By sin we can place ourselves in a position where we cannot gain anything from it, but the promise itself can never be taken back: it is as irrevocable as the natural order which God has bound Himself to preserve. And it is because it sees things in this light that Christian thought has such deep-rooted optimism.

But at the same time, beside God's fidelity in the Old Testament, we come upon this second reality—the infidelity of His people. Although, on the one hand, nothing can prevent God's plan from being carried out, on the other we are faced with the terrible power man's freedom gives him of setting a barrier to it; he cannot stop its existing, but he can prevent it from bearing fruit. And it is this side of things that the history of Israel shows us; God is constantly urging His people to serve Him, and the people are as constantly being unfaithful, and, by their faithlessness, drawing away from God's gifts. There are splendid passages in the prophets, particularly Ezechiel, reminding the people of their infidelities, and beseeching them to return to goodness. Even there in the very heart of the Bible we find once more this double view of historical continuity coupled with a tragic opposition.

Contemporary thought is giving us a degraded version of this Biblical opposition when it shows us at once an optimistic historical view of things and a despairing dramatic one. We have, on the one hand, that immense faith in material progress which has given rise to a movement like communism. The root of communist thought, as we find it in the Marxian philosophy on which it is based, is the idea that through history there is some progress being irrevocably accomplished. There may be crises, there may be revolutions. But they are mere episodes within this great "becoming" which covers hundreds of thousands of years, through which the progress is taking place. We need therefore do nothing but put our faith in history, our trust in progress; we may not see it, what matters is that it is happening.

This is a horrible parody of a great Christian idea: it is the Christian faith in a City of God, a faith founded on God's own promise, which is in communism debased into hope for a perfect earthly city, built by the hands of men. And we must be careful, in criticising thought like this of the Communists, that what we are rejecting is the perversion, and not the heritage, the parody and not the Christian thought. Faith in the meaning of history, the deep faith that in all the revolutions and all the tragedies we have gone through something is maturing, something is being formed and going forward towards good, is an essentially Christian view. It is a duty for us today, amongst all the despair and all the apparent illusion, to preserve this fundamental optimism, and to preserve it not merely as *much* as everyone else, but *more*, because we know more than the rest how, throughout all the dramas, the City of God is mysteriously building up, in other ways than those we know, but with a certainty nothing can alter, because God is faithful to His promise. We know that the Word of God is at work in the world, carrying out His plan, and that this plan will be completed without fail, and that all nations will one day be reunited in the kingdom of the Father.

At the same time—and here you have the paradox—there is a current in contemporary thought which goes in exactly the opposite direction, which thinks the world is essentially absurd, and our only possible attitude a sort of despairing humanism, which, seeing the absurdity of everything, cannot have hope, because all hope is an illusion, but tries to handle things as well as possible so as to preserve a minimum of human happiness. That is what Camus, for instance, is after. Clearly the world in which we live gives every appearance of justifying this notion from many points of view; for it is obvious that its situation is highly absurd, and that we are caught up in a series of contradictions and complexities not governed by reason. And it is easy to understand how men's minds can find the best expression of this fact in a philosophy of absurdity and despair.

There again we come upon a Christian idea being

parodied—the Christian pessimism of Pascal and Kierkegaard, which is the realisation of the disorder in the world.
But Christians do not see this disorder as of the nature of
things; it is caused by man's sinful use of his liberty, by
which he introduces evil into the harmonious work of God.
The criticism made by existentialists of Marxists drives
home when they show how naïve communist optimism is,
because it completely fails to understand this fundamental
reality—the terrifying power of human freedom. Material
elements alone do not determine human destiny. Man's
free will is independent of material causality; that is its
greatness, in this it resembles the divine, from this comes
its terrible power of doing evil or good. This is the element
not to be foreseen, the only one that does not fit into
the communist scheme, yet sufficient by itself to make it
fail. Now we know that there is only one thing that can
have any power over this freedom: there is another and
higher freedom to which it must submit or deny its own
nature.

We have now gathered the principles we need to solve
the problem, stated at the beginning, of Christianity's
relationship to other religions. It has a double relation to
them, historic and dramatic. In the first place, beside
the other civilisations Christianity is essentially something
new. Vaillant-Couturier said: "Communism is the youth
of the world." Yet another parody on a great Christian
idea! I think it would be hard to find a more exact definition of Christianity: Christianity is the eternal youth
of the world. There are those today who suffer at the
thought that Christianity may have been left behind,
have grown old. This may be true of certain things which
have grown out of it, exterior to it, but never of its essence:
Christianity is, and always will be, the youth of the world

because it comes exactly chronologically at the end of the development of history. And the true relation of Christianity to all other religions is this—that they all come before it, they are all outworn. I do not say they are completely false: Judaism, Buddhism, the fetishist civilisations are not so much false as *old*: that is to say, they belong to the time before Christianity, and are, in some way, survivals; Christianity which perfects them has come, and henceforth all that was good in them is fulfilled in it. We look at them together, we see the juxtaposition in space of things which follow each other in the historical order of time, and it is an odd thing that they can actually exist simultaneously, and therefore be connected as two things present at once, though their essential connection is by succession.

Why is this? With Judaism it is clear enough. Obviously Judaism was directed solely towards the coming of Christianity. But it is equally true of the non-Christian religions. They are not so much false as essentially incomplete, unfinished. Remember what Saint Irenaeus said: God made man familiar with certain natural truths, with a certain sense of God. But these civilisations have remained at this stage of development and have not opened themselves to the fulness of Revelation. Then there are others, such as Islam, which must be called regressions; they have abandoned certain aspects of Christianity, as if things were going too fast for them, to get back to that idea of pedagogy, as if there were races or men who were not yet able to bear the fulness of Revelation.

What characterises Christianity is a certain wholeness; in it there is the fulness of truth. In the order of *continuity* it marks a more advanced stage of evolution, the highest point of that evolution. I believe this idea to be absolutely essential if we are to understand how Christianity completes other religions and other civilisations, and to see as a result that everlasting newness, which Saint Augustine and so many others have proclaimed. Christianity is and always will be "the newest thing out". "You are the most modern man alive," said Guillaume Apollinaire to Pope Pius X, as if he had a sort of intuition of this eternal newness of Christianity.

You see where the dramatic relation between Christianity and the non-Christian civilisations has to come in. Between it and them there will be opposition to the extent that they refuse to let themselves be superseded. As Origen said so well, in regard to the Jews who resisted Christ: "It was the figure clinging to life by fighting the reality which fulfilled it." This is also true of us when we refuse to lay ourselves open to the developing demands of grace; sin is always the thing that paralyses us, that turns us back on ourselves. The special mark of these civilisations is that they have turned back on themselves; they refuse to open out. The Jewish people refused to open themselves to Christ; they refused that death which would have opened to them a far greater scope for living, they turned in upon their own riches and became unable to receive the new riches offered them. And, indeed, it is true that in the renunciation required there is something which makes it a hard thing for any civilisation.

This willingness to be superseded is absolutely necessary, as Saint Irenaeus explains so beautifully: "Just as the branch on the vine is not made for its own sake, but for the cluster of grapes growing on it; and the grapes once ripe, the branch is cast away as useless, so with Jerusalem. It bore the yoke of slavery, and once the fruit of freedom had appeared and ripened and been picked and stored, then it was only right that what had hitherto borne the fruit should be left behind." The civilisation of Israel had borne its fruit, and the fruit was Christ, and when once the fruit was there, what further need for the branch? Once the grapes are ripe and can be enjoyed, the branch becomes valueless; all the good that was in it is now in the grapes. And, since the figure of this whole world must pass away at the time prepared for it, what does Jerusalem matter as long as its fruit is gathered? The whole world was also made to ripen a fruit—the City of God—and when the fruit is ripe, then this world can pass away as an old garment is folded up, as the cocoon drops away from the fully formed butterfly.

This is especially true of pagan civilisations: for them, to open themselves to Christ would simply mean to bear the fruit, and therefore, in a sense, to throw away the branch. They have many outworn forms which they would have to agree to do away with; in fact it is a mystery of death alongside the mystery of life, a mystery of renunciation, and indeed of old age, alongside the mystery of newness. They would have to accept life; but the trouble is that the new life is too much for the old framework, the new wine will burst the old bottles; we feel it in our own souls—the new wine of grace is forever bursting the old bottles we want to put it in, forcing us to grow beyond our own limits—for we are always trying to build up our own kind of compromise—and to go on to the next stage.

What is true of the development of an individual soul is true of the development of a nation. That is what is hard to accept, and that is where the civilisation will tend to turn back on itself, its senility, its avarice: avarice is indeed the major obstacle to grace. There is always a problem of growth and a problem of life: it is the life of God trying to fashion mankind, and mankind's resistance, refusing life, fighting against growth, and thus not attaining full development. These general principles will help us to work out the relationship between Christianity and the non-Christian worlds. When we have arrived at that, then perhaps we can see better how we may most usefully serve God's plan.

PART I
THE FIRST PRECURSORS

I

ABRAHAM AND THE HEBREW COVENANT

THE Old Testament is the story of how God educated mankind to be able to receive the divine gifts He destined for them. Before He came in the flesh and accomplished fully the mystery of the salvation of the world, and the mystery of the salvation of the nations, the Word of God Himself began by preparing His ways in history. As a first step towards this, God chose Abraham and his race to tell them something of the mystery of Christ, in a way obscure and hidden, but none the less quite real. Men's minds were utterly crude and materialist, and His method was to raise them bit by bit—here Saint Irenaeus' words take on their full force—from the worship of idols to a point where they could understand and in part foresee the realities Christ was to bring, so that when Christ at last appeared, and His mystery was revealed, men would be able to understand Him. Had He been presented to them too suddenly they could not have been.[1]

From our standpoint, seeing Abraham as one of those who prepared the way of the Lord, three lines of study suggest themselves:

First, it was he who started the preparation, so that in his vocation there was something unique, and his setting out was the beginning of something wholly new.

Then there are the great sacraments, the great mysteries of Abraham's life, which we shall show to be sacraments of Our Lord, that is, prefigurations of His life.

[1] See Suzanne de Dietrich, *Le Dessein de Dieu*, 1945; A. G. Hebert, *The Authority of the Scriptures*, 1947.

We shall consider the three great sacraments—the word is used by the Fathers of the Church to describe these figures of the Old Testament: the covenant, a figure of the New Testament and the Covenant of Christ; the miraculous birth of Isaac, a figure of the Virgin Birth of Jesus; and, lastly, the marriage of Isaac and Rebecca, in which the Fathers saw a figure of the marriage of Christ with His Church.

Lastly, we shall try to fit Abraham's life into the setting of a theology of history, showing Abraham's special relation to the Jewish people, the Mahomedans and the Christians, which makes of his life a figure of the succession of peoples in God's plan, and of the evangelisation of the whole world.

1. *Abraham's Vocation*

Chapter xii of Genesis tells us how Abraham, son of Thare, left Haran in northern Syria, to go into the land of Chanaan, at the command of God: "And the Lord said to Abraham: Go forth out of thy country, and from thy kindred, and out of thy father's house, and come into the land which I shall show thee. And I will make of thee a great nation, and I will bless thee, and magnify thy name . . . And in thee shall all the kindred of the earth be blessed" (xii. 1-3). This event is one that we can quite easily fit into its historical context. Ur, in Chaldea, whence Abraham's father had set out, Haran in northern Syria, and the land of Chanaan, were three important centres situated in the "fertile crescent" around the north of the Syrian desert. This region was inhabited at about 3000 B.C. by Semites, the ancestors of the Arabs and the Jews, many of whom were Bedouin nomads. At this time certain of the tribes were constantly migrating. The migration of Thare and Abraham is an example of this. They left Ur, the wealthy Chaldean city. They stayed for some time at Haran. And they finally came to the land of Chanaan, which was inhabited by Semites; the latter were related to the Phoenicians of whose civilisation and worship we have learnt a great deal from excavations.[1]

Yet this migration, which can be placed as a not specially remarkable historical event, was at the same time an almost unique happening, paralleled only by the Creation of the world, and Christ's Incarnation. It was in fact the first beginning of God's action in history, just as the Creation was the beginning of His action upon the cosmos, and the Incarnation the beginning of the world to come. It marks the opening of sacred history—perhaps indeed of all history. It is the first appearance of historical action by the living God. With it came a new order of reality which was to fill nineteen centuries. And it is this which gives Abraham's setting-out its unique character. The rest of the Old Testament was, like him, to prepare for and prefigure Christ. But it belonged to him alone to start the work.

There are several aspects of this event. It was, first, an order to leave, to separate. What God commanded Abraham was, in fact, to start something absolutely new, which implied a break with all that had been before in the religious sphere. Indeed, up to then, Scripture seems to tell us, Abraham had shared in the idolatrous beliefs of his people: "Your fathers dwelt of old on the other side of the river [Ur was in Mesopotamia]: Thare the father of Abraham and Nachor. And they served strange gods" (Josue xxiv. 2; cf. Judith v. 8). Abraham's

---

[1] See R. de Langhe, *Les textes de Ras Shamra et leurs rapports avec le milieu biblique de l'Ancien Testament*, 1945.

departure was therefore a breaking away from idols, and the inauguration of the worship of the true God. We may note, in passing, that this aspect of Abraham's life was particularly stressed by Mahomed in the Koran.[1] Mahomed, who had himself to fight the polytheism of the Arab tribes, glorified the man who, twenty-six centuries earlier, had inaugurated monotheism, and rejected idolatrous cults not far different from those he himself was faced with. And, indeed, what Abraham was inaugurating was the revealed monotheism which has remained the common treasure of three great spiritual families who recognise him to be their ancestor: the Jews, the Mahomedans, and the Christians.

This setting forth of Abraham's has echoed through all subsequent religious history. In Jewish-Christian tradition he is the model and archetype of conversion to the living God in the first total act of faith. The Old Testament constantly recurs to this as the origin of the Jewish people's vocation. The New Testament makes him the very pattern of faith: "By faith he that is called Abraham obeyed to go out into a place which he was to receive for an inheritance. And he went out not knowing whither he went" (Heb. xi. 8). The Jewish theologian Philo devoted one of his treatises to the *Migratio Abrahae*,[2] in which he saw a symbol of man's soul leaving visible things to go forward to invisible. Gregory of Nyssa shows him to us as the model of the soul setting out towards God in the darkness of faith, and in a brilliant commentary on the Epistle to the Hebrews he says in regard to Abraham's "not knowing whither he went" that it was precisely "because he did not know whither he went that he knew

---

[1] *Koran*, Sura 21.
[2] The translation of this excellent text by R. Cadiou will soon be published in the *Universités de France* collection (Soc. Guillaume Budé).

he was going right, for then he was certain that he was not being led by the light of his own mind, but by the will of God"[1] Pascal's conversion, on that decisive night, was to be conversion "to the God of Abraham, Isaac and Jacob, not the God of the philosophers and scholars". To Kierkegaard, and to Chestov, "the perfect thinker was Abraham, the father of faith, and not Socrates. To Abraham faith was a new dimension of thought, which the world did not yet know, which had no place in ordinary knowledge, and simply broke through the restraining truths of our experience and our reason".[2] And Jean Hering could write: "The model for a Christian is not the princess in exile who longs to return; it is Abraham setting out towards an unknown country to be shown him by God."[3]

But while Abraham's election was an order to leave, a break with the past, it was also a promise, the announcement of things to come. Thus it appeared from the start what was to be the character of the new religion. Cosmic religion recognised God's action in the regularity of the stars' courses and the seasons which God had guaranteed by the covenant He made with Noe (Gen. ix. 9–17): it was a religion of nature. The religion of the Bible, on the other hand, was to be a waiting for historical happenings of the future. The Epistle to the Hebrews gives an incomparable explanation of this aspect of the promise given to Abraham: "For God making promise to Abraham, because he had no one greater by whom he might swear, swore by himself, saying: Unless blessing I shall bless thee, and multiplying I shall multiply thee. And so patiently enduring, he obtained the promise. . . .

---

[1] *Contra Eunomium*, xxii; P. G. xliv. 940, B.D.
[2] Chestov, *Athens and Jerusalem*, p. 347.
[3] *Le Royaume de Dieu et sa venue*, p. 150.

Wherein God, meaning more abundantly to show to the heirs of the promise the immutability of his counsel, interposed an oath: that by two immutable things in which it is impossible for God to lie, we may have the strongest comfort, we who have fled for refuge to hold fast the hope set before us. Which we have as an anchor of the soul, sure and firm, which entereth in even within the veil: where the forerunner Jesus is entered for us" (Heb. vi. 13–20). We still have this hope of Abraham's, but for us it does not rest purely on God's irrevocable faithfulness to His word, but also on the reality we already possess of the union of Godhead and manhood in Christ which can never be broken, and on the fact that by His Ascension He introduced the humanity to which He had united Himself into the life of the Trinity forever. This is the reality that we can cling to with all our might, so that we may pass unshaken through all life's trials, waiting as heirs for the day of our entry into the enjoyment of the goods which Christ won for our nature and which in Him we already possess. Yet in fact all this glory is simply the development of the first promise made to Abraham.

The mysterious object of that promise was the salvation of the nations. "All the kindred of the earth shall be blessed in thee." What is extraordinary here is that at the very beginning of sacred history its end should be set before him. That end, which is the end of the whole of creation—that is to say, that all spiritual beings were created to recognise and give glory to the Blessed Trinity: *Adveniat regnum tuum*—was set before Abraham as early as this. It was, of course, to be unfolded over the long course of the centuries, through God's great works in the threefold history of Israel, Christ and the Church. And this threefold history itself was the object of Abraham's faith:

he was called upon to believe that he would be "the father of a mighty nation" though his wife Sara was barren; that in his seed, that is, through one of his descendants, God's blessing would be spread over all mankind, which meant that the Messias would be a descendant of his—"Abraham rejoiced that he might see my day," Jesus was to say of him (John viii. 56[1]); and lastly that all the kindred of the earth should be saved, which meant the founding of the Church.[2] But from the beginning, the object of God's promise and the object of Abraham's faith was the salvation of the nations —in fact the very object of missionary work. Thus what Abraham waited for so long ago we still await. And just as he, alone in an utterly pagan world, believed that all nations should be saved, so, sticking to our faith, even when everything seems to point against it, we must continue to wait, in the Advent of the Church, for all nations to be gathered together in Him who took His flesh in one of Abraham's daughters.

We can understand, then, why Saint Paul, the Apostle of the Gentiles, so often showed how the promise made to Abraham was being fulfilled in his mission. It is not to the Law, which was only a provisory arrangement for the education of the Jews, but to the promise made to Abraham, that he always refers. This promise, though it was given at the beginning of the Old Testament, had awaited fulfilment for a very long time, for much preparation was needed; but it was now being fulfilled in the missionary work of the Church: "And the Scripture, foreseeing that God justifieth the gentiles by faith, told unto Abraham before: In thee shall all nations be blessed"

[1] See the commentary by F. C. Hoskyns, *The Fourth Gospel*, p. 245.
[2] "By faith he abode in the land of promise as in a strange country . . . for he looked for a city that hath foundations, whose builder and maker is God" (Heb. xi. 9–10).

(Gal. iii. 8). This good news which was given to Abraham is called in the Greek text of Saint Paul *evangelion*, the Gospel, *the* good news. It was this gospel that Abraham knew, and after the long delay ordained by God's wisdom Paul was now its herald. The same gospel is still being preached in the era of grace represented by the present world; now, through His Church, God officially proclaims that all nations are admitted to salvation. This evangelisation will be complete only at the end of time. Indeed Scripture teaches again and again that "this gospel of the kingdom shall be preached in the whole world . . . and then shall the consummation come" (Matt. xxiv. 14). The salvation of the nations, then, is still an object of faith and expectation, as it was for Abraham. But just as Christ's raising people from the dead prefigured the final resurrection of the Last Day—and, as K. L. Schmidt remarks with such depth, the very fact that those who had been raised died again shows that their raising was merely a figure—so for one unique moment in history, on the day of Pentecost, the Holy Ghost united all the nations represented in Jerusalem in one common language and thus fulfilled in figure, and, as it were, in seed, the promise to Abraham, which will be made good at the end of time.

This salvation of the nations is "the mystery hidden from eternity in God who created all things", the restoring of all things in Christ. Saint Paul was to say that it was to him, "the least of all the saints", that it was given "to enlighten all men" that they might see this mystery (Eph. iii. 8–9). But Abraham before him had been the first to hear. And that is his unique grandeur. On the threshold of sacred history, he was the first to whom God told the secret of His plans, to whom He entrusted the knowledge of His mysterious ways. That is why he is the first of the prophets[1] For prophecy is the understanding of the mystery of sacred history given by the Holy Spirit who alone fathoms the depths of God. The mystery of history is summed up in God's design of giving His spiritual creatures a share in the life of the Trinity. Now that is a secret as mysterious as God Himself, and even the angels cannot see into its depths. Only the Spirit, who brings the design to accomplishment, can give anyone an understanding of it. Abraham beheld it. God unfolded before his eyes His *magnalia*, the great works which He does, and which are the reality of history, as God accomplishes it through the ages. For that *is* the promise— the manifestation of an irrevocable design, when faith leans, unsupported by experience, on a reality firmer than anything perceived by sense, because it is actually based on fidelity to God. Abraham beheld these *magnalia*. His soul faltered before their incomprehensible grandeur, as under a weight too heavy, heavier than flesh could bear. And Scripture tells us that he was seized by a kind of ecstasy or loss of his senses (*tardemah*), "a great and darksome horror" (Gen. xv. 12). Remember Adam at the beginning, when the mystery of Christ and the Church was revealed to him, too, in the creation of woman, and an ecstasy (*tardemah*) fell on him, for "this is a great sacrament" (Eph. v. 32). But, at the same time, Christ tells us, his soul exulted too at the beauty of this design. And remember, too, that other day, when a daughter of Abraham, struck with wonder by the glory of what God, in carrying out the promise given to Abraham—*sicut locutus est ad Abraham Patrem nostrum*—had wrought in her, also exulted, and, raised by the spirit of prophecy above the smallness of earthly things, proclaimed the grandeur

---

[1] "Since Abraham was a prophet and saw in spirit the coming of the Lord, he exulted in his soul" (Irenaeus, *Adv. haer.*, iv, 5, 5).

of God's works with that cry of wonder which has come down the ages: *Magnificat anima mea Dominum, et exultavit spiritus meus in Deo salutari meo.*

These great works of His, God continues to carry out in the world, and we do not see them, because our mind is on other things. We, too, need John the Baptist to cry to us: "There hath stood one in the midst of you, whom you know not." We need the Holy Spirit, who performs these tremendous works of God, to give us understanding, and to lead us beyond the history we can see, to contemplate true history. These works, which are hidden from the eyes of our body, are what the Holy Spirit does in the sacraments, which are a continuation among us of God's great works in the Old and New Testament. As God set His people in Egypt free at the first Pasch, as He liberated Christ from death on the second Pasch, so on the third Pasch, our Easter, he sets free by baptism souls enslaved to sin. In the same way, through the Eucharist, He is forever among us giving glory to His Father. And these are realities far beyond any the world wonders at. These are realities far greater than victories or revolutions, than any discovered by scholars, than anything created by artistic genius, inasmuch as the order of charity outweighs the order of flesh and the order of intelligence. These are works wrought in the secret of men's hearts, works whereby men are converted, sanctified and divinised. And that is how, in the secrecy of quiet lives we do not even see, the incorruptible body of Christ is being formed in charity, and It alone will defy the fires of judgment when all the straw of human deeds goes up in flames. Only the Holy Spirit can effect incorruptibility.

What the missionary soul contemplates are the great works of God. The Holy Spirit draws souls living hidden lives away from all care for things of this earth, from the world of appearances, and takes them into the real world, which is founded on God's faithfulness to His Word. With Abraham, with Mary, with Paul and all the saints, they marvel at the irrevocable unfolding of God's plan. And God, by purifying His works in this way, makes them fit to be His tools. So Abraham left his family and his country, that he might be of use in the design God was to inaugurate with him, so Mary answered Gabriel's announcement with a *Fiat*. It was not a question of contemplation followed by action. These souls were seized by the divine reality and used as its tools. But here again Abraham has a unique position in that he inaugurated missionary contemplation. For us this contemplation takes in both the past and the future. And the past is even greater than the future to us for whom the thing that matters most has already happened—Godhead has been united inseparably and forever with humanity in Jesus Christ. But for Abraham, all God's work lay in the future. His faith had to bear the burden of all the future unaided by any sign from the past. And we can understand how he was overwhelmed by such a weight, as Jesus was in the Garden of Olives,[1] and yet "in the promise of God he staggered not by distrust: but was strengthened in faith, giving glory to God: most fully knowing that whatsoever he has promised, he is able also to perform. And therefore it was reputed to him unto justice" (Rom. iv. 20–2).

2. *Isaac*

Abraham was henceforward the instrument of God's plans. By his faith in the promise he had inaugurated sacred history; he went on to perform the first actions in

[1] S. de Dietrich, *op. cit.*, p. 46.

that history. And because God is constant in His ways, the great deeds done by Abraham were not only the first steps leading up to Christ, but also the first figures of the mysteries He was to accomplish. Indeed, the whole of the Old Testament is a prefiguration of the New, inasmuch as through the events it relates we see dimly those same ways of God which the New Testament manifests so much more clearly. In the Flood, for instance, we see mankind, wholly enslaved to sin, being punished and one just man spared to be the source of a new humanity. Abraham's story gives us some of the greatest of such "sacraments". They are listed in the Epistle to the Hebrews: "By faith he abode in the land of promise as in a strange country, dwelling in cottages, with Isaac and Jacob, the co-heirs of the same promise. For he looked for a city that hath foundations, whose builder and maker is God." This is the mystery of the old covenant, the figure of the New Covenant. "By faith also Sara herself, being barren, received strength to conceive seed, even past the time of age: because she believed that he was faithful who had promised." This is the mystery of Isaac being born of a barren woman, the figure of Jesus being born of a virgin. "By faith Abraham, when he was tried, offered Isaac: and he that had received the promises offered up his only begotten son; (to whom it was said: In Isaac shall thy seed be called): accounting that God is able to raise up even from the dead. Whereupon also he received him for a *parable*" (Heb. xi. 9-11, 17-19). Here the text itself says that the sacrifice of Isaac was a figure of Christ's resurrection— that is to say, salvation accomplished through apparent failure.

The first of these sacraments was the covenant itself. Abraham was the first man with whom God made a personal covenant. It was an event essential to the history of the world. You might say that until the coming of Christ it was the most important thing that happened, and that is what gives Abraham his outstanding place in the religious history of man, a place recognised not only by Christians but also by Jews and Mahomedans; a place outstanding in the history of mankind because this was the first time God had intervened in history to bind mankind to Himself in a special bond. God was choosing, electing by His grace, a people, and first of all a man, Abraham, in such a way as to enter into the closest and most familiar relations with him. There you have the very essence of faith. To believe is to hold that God does things of this sort. Men do not believe if they think in a general way that God exists, but do not for one moment think that God takes any part in history.

The covenant was, then, a bond set up between God and Abraham. But it is important to understand what kind of bond it was. It was not a bilateral contract by which two parties are so bound that if either fails in his engagements, the other is absolved from keeping his. Saint Paul seems to reject such an interpretation of the word (Gal. iii. 17–18). The Hebrew word *berith* which is used for this contract can be translated by *syntheke*, or covenant; but Paul translates it by *diatheke*, which means testament. Thence comes the double term Old Covenant and Old Testament. Now the word testament is more exact. The covenant was in fact a divine disposition whereby God freely shared what belonged to Him with a people because He had chosen them, and not because they had any right to it. And just as they had not earned it by any right, so no breach of faith on their part could cause it to be taken away. They may so act that they will not reap the fruits of the covenant, but they can never cause it to be revoked. Thus we are led to the notion of an unchanging order which is also an order of grace. It is this double aspect which gives this covenant its uniqueness. And this order is also utterly irrevocable. Man can always claim it. He need only turn to it, and he will get its effects. That is why whenever the people of Israel prayed they always begged God to remember the covenant He had made with Abraham and not reject the people to whom He had given His promise (Exod. ii. 24; Ps. lxxxviii, 4).

It was then, on God's part, an irrevocable, unchangeable promise, given forever. And this is an anticipation and figure of grace. What exactly is the grace of the New Testament? It is that henceforth and forever there shall be a bond between mankind and God which can never be broken, because it is founded on the manhood of Christ, in whom Godhead and manhood are henceforth joined together forever. This can never be broken. Christ has brought our humanity into the inmost life of God to stay. Can we, then (and this is the thing that matters),— can we withdraw from grace? This brings us back to what I said in my Introduction; we can withdraw ourselves from it, but it can never be done away with. This is the real mystery of the covenant. God is not absolved from being faithful by our faithlessness. God does not cease to be faithful because we are unfaithful. He is faithful in spite of our infidelities. We may fail to gain anything from the promise, but the promise itself will never be revoked. We can always appeal to it.[1] The promise made to Abraham is a figure of this: whatever the infidelities and sins of Israel, however often they turned to idols, God would never take back His promise, and the whole

---

[1] This is explained by the *character* given by baptism. The covenant once contracted at baptism, though one may lose the grace of baptism by serious sin, one can never lose the right to receive it again as soon as one has returned to the proper dispositions.

history of Israel was to be the history of the covenant—
that is to say, of the fidelity of God, and the infidelity of
Israel. The history of Israel prefigures the state of things
to be between mankind and Christ: the fidelity of God
which ends by wearing out our infidelities. This is the
mystery of God's patience. If He let go of us when we
were unfaithful, He would have let go of us long ago. But
He will never let go. It is thus that He shows us His love.
A promise once given, He will never go back on. We can
stop ourselves gaining anything from it, but we cannot
get away from it. All that is deepest in the New Testament
mysteries concerning this had already begun to be brought
about in the Old.

This promise God made to Abraham He sanctioned by a
rite, a document which signified it, and so was a kind of
sacrament of it, and which would at the same time abide
as a reminder in later times: "The Lord . . . said to him:
Look up to heaven, and number the stars, if thou canst.
And he said to him: So shall thy seed be"—that was the
promise—"Abraham believed God, and it was reputed
to him unto justice". That is the text Saint Paul used
in the Epistle to the Romans. "And He said to him:
I am the Lord who brought thee out from Ur of the
Chaldees. . . . Take me a cow of three years old, and a
she-goat of three years, and a ram of three years, a turtle
also, and a pigeon. And he took all these and divided
them in the midst, and laid the two pieces of each one
against the other; but the birds he divided not. . . . And
when the sun was setting, a deep sleep fell upon Abram:
and a great and darksome horror seized upon him. And
it was said unto him: Know thou beforehand that thy
seed shall be a stranger in a land not their own . . . And
when the sun was set, there arose a dark mist; and there
appeared a smoking furnace, and a lamp of fire passing

between those divisions. That day God made a covenant with Abraham saying: To thy seed will I give this land, from the river of Egypt even to the great river Euphrates" (Gen. xv. 5–6, 7, 9–10, 12–13, 17–18).

A mysterious rite, and we find the same sort of thing elsewhere in the Old Testament: the covenant is symbolised by a divided victim. This is a sign that those who have thus shared the same blood are united in a bond of alliance; and a rite of this kind was often used in the world in ancient times to symbolise a covenant. Whenever two peoples made alliance, they would make an exchange of blood to symbolise this unity. God was here using an analogous symbol to be a sort of visible sacrament of this alliance. Abraham and God thus divided the victims, and the lamp of fire, which symbolised the presence of the Lord Himself, passed between them, and in some way sanctified the sacrament.[1] In the same way, later on in the Old Testament, we see fire coming from God falling on the victims to consume them: and you remember how, in the Mass, we pray the Holy Spirit to descend on the victim to consecrate it: it is God's acceptance of the victim. We have here, then, a sacrament of the covenant. And we recall that there is also a sacrament of the New Covenant; just as in the Old Testament the covenant was symbolised by the dividing of the victim and its blood, so there is a sacrament, a charter of the New Covenant, to succeed the *antiquum documentum* the *Tantum ergo* speaks of; it also is the blood of an immolated Victim which the Gospel calls "blood of the New Testament", and it was this that the ancient rite of the covenant with Abraham prefigured.

In each case we have a sacrament which is a figure of the

---

[1] The fact that it is the Lord who passes between the victims is a sign that He is the one who is making the covenant.

promise and which remains with us as a visible reminder. We do not often refer to this meaning of the Eucharist— that it is a witness which reminds us of our covenant with God, an everlasting memorial which forbids us to forget. Though mankind could forget for nineteen centuries, the Eucharist is still there, visibly reminding us of the New Covenant, just as sacrifice helped the Jews to remember the former covenant. And because the covenant is the great proof of God's love, it is of love that this is a memorial.

The second sacrament is most important, because it corresponds to one of those points in the Catholic faith about which difficulties are oftenest made, I mean the Virgin Birth. It shows that Christ's being born of a virgin was not some kind of aberration, something totally unconnected with everything else. During the course of the Old Testament God had been preparing men's minds to understand it. If this miracle of the Virgin Birth had suddenly happened, with no sort of preparation made for it, men could not have accepted it. Why were they able to understand it? Because when the angel Gabriel appeared to Mary he told her she should conceive a son who would be the Son of the Most High. This awoke an echo in Our Lady's soul. She remembered other annunciations: in the Old Testament angels had appeared to women to tell them they would bear children by the power of God. None of those were virginal births, but were cases where women who had long been barren conceived children by the power of God. That was a miracle of a lower order, which prefigured the infinitely greater miracle by which the Virgin, Our Lady, conceived a son without having known man. We shall always find such a difference between the figure and the reality: the figure in the Old Testament was a copy, but always a lesser copy, of the New.

Now this took place for the very first time in the history of Abraham and Sara. Sara, Abraham's wife, was barren. But God had promised Abraham that from him would come a great nation. He believed this, despite the seeming impossibility. It is absolutely necessary to the nature of faith to rest on the power of God and not the experience of man. Saint Paul glorified this faith: "Who against hope believed in hope; that he might be made the father of many nations, according to that which was said to him: So shall thy seed be. And he was not weak in faith. Neither did he consider his own body, now dead (whereas he was almost a hundred years old), nor the dead womb of Sara. In the promise also of God he staggered not by distrust: but was strengthened in faith, giving glory to God" (Rom. iv. 18–20; cf. Heb. xi. 11–12).

It is here that Agar and Ismael come in. Abraham, seeing that Sara could not have a child, took a concubine, Agar;[1] by her he had Ismael, who is the father of Islam. But this child was not the child of the promise, as Abraham was later to understand. That is why the Lord appeared to Sara. That was the first Annunciation: "And the Lord visited Sara as he had promised: and fulfilled what he had spoken. And she conceived and bore a son in her old age, at the time that God had foretold her. . . . And Sara said: God hath made a laughter for me. Whoever shall hear of it will laugh with me. . . . And the Lord said to Abraham: . . . In Isaac shall thy seed be called" (Gen. xxi. 1–2, 6, 12).

There we have one birth resulting from God's intervention. And it is not the only case in the Old Testament. We find it again further on. At the beginning of the first

---

[1] As to how we may reconcile Abraham's holiness with this polygamy, see the enlightening comments of Raïssa Maritain in *Histoire d'Abraham ou les étapes de la conscience morale*, 1947, pp. 5 ff.

Book of Kings (Samuel) we find Anna, Samuel's mother, in great misery because she is sterile, and going to pray in the temple, and a messenger from God appears to tell her she will have a child. And she sings a canticle which is a prototype of the *Magnificat*:

> My heart hath rejoiced in the Lord . . . my mouth is enlarged over my enemies, because I have joyed in thy salvation. . . . He raiseth up the needy from the dust, and lifteth up the poor from the dunghill: that he may sit with princes and hold the throne of glory (1 Kings ii. 1, 8).

By these successive manifestations God accustomed men to the idea of miraculous births, so that the miracle of the Virgin Birth would not seem a totally new departure, but would fit into a certain pattern and thus be to some extent understood. What is intelligibility? It means that a fact can be placed in relation to a series of other facts. There is, of course, one kind of intelligibility when a thing can be understood by reason. But there is also a kind of intelligibility proper to Revelation by which the events of the New Testament can be placed in relationship with those of the Old and do not suddenly appear unrelated to anything we know, as from a world utterly strange to us. It makes the Virgin Birth intelligible by showing it in relation to the Old Testament.

The third sacrament was the sacrifice of Isaac. The further forward we go, the more we enter into the very heart of the mystery of Christ. . We come here to a high point in the Old Testament. Let me begin by saying that this sacrifice of Isaac held an important place in Jewish thought. It was what they called the *hakeda*. In the first centuries of the Christian era the rabbis taught that

Abraham merited all the graces given later to his people by sacrificing Isaac, and that Isaac, by submitting to be sacrificed, was the cause of his people's salvation. This teaching must certainly have been influenced by Saint Paul's showing that Christ gave His life for His people. But the importance they gave to the sacrifice itself dates back to much earlier.[1] The theme of the sacrifice of Isaac is also dear to Mahomedan piety. It is mentioned several times in the Koran as having been the supreme proof of Abraham's faith.

Let us first read the chapter in Genesis:

And after these things God tempted Abraham, and said to him: Abraham, Abraham. And he answered: Here I am. He said to him: Take thy only-begotten son Isaac, whom thou lovest, and go into the land of vision.

We find in Saint Paul the idea that "the Father gave his only-begotten Son". He was clearly thinking of that chapter in Genesis where Abraham also gave his only-begotten son. The sacrifice of Abraham was a figure of the sacrifice made by the Father of Him who was the one Only-begotten, the Christ. . . .

So Abraham, rising up in the night, saddled his ass: and took with him two young men, and Isaac his son. . . . And he took the wood for the holocaust, and laid it upon Isaac his son. . . . And as they two went on together, Isaac said to his father: My father. And he answered: What wilt thou, son? Behold, saith he, fire and wood; where is the victim for the holocaust? . . . And they came to the place which God had shown

[1] See *La typologie d'Isaac dans le christianisme primitif*, Biblica 1947, pp. 363 ff.

him, where he built an altar, and laid the wood in order upon it. And when he had bound Isaac his son, he laid him upon the altar, on the pile of wood. And he put forth his hand and took the sword to sacrifice his son. And behold, an angel of the Lord from heaven called to him, saying: Abraham, Abraham. And he answered: Here I am. And he said to him: Lay not thy hand upon the boy, neither do thou any thing to him. Now I know that thou fearest God and hast not spared thy only-begotten son for my sake. Abraham lifted up his eyes, and saw behind his back a ram amongst the briers sticking fast by the horns, which he took and offered for a holocaust.

And let us then re-read the passage from the Epistle to the Hebrews which sees the full meaning of this:

By faith Abraham, when he was tried, offered Isaac: and he that had received the promises offered up his only begotten son; (to whom it was said: In Isaac shall thy seed be called): accounting that God is able to raise up even from the dead (Heb. xi. 17–19).

We see the difference between this sacrifice of Isaac and Christ's sacrifice: the former was not consummated. It belonged to the figures in the Old Testament to adumbrate, but not to accomplish fully. Saint Paul gives us another striking example, that of the High Priest entering the Holy of Holies once a year. The very fact that it was repeated every year shows well enough that it was only a figure, that it was not as yet the reality, whereas Christ entered *once and for all* into the true Holy of Holies. In just the same way Isaac, offered but not immolated, is a shadowy sketch of Christ who was immolated in very fact;

and, as the Epistle to the Hebrews remarks with such depth, Isaac given back to his father still alive, not risen from the dead, is a figure of Christ risen.

What makes this episode such a very impressive figure of the Passion of Christ is that here, too, we see apparent failure becoming the cause of the promise being fulfilled. God promised Abraham that He would make Isaac a mighty nation, and He then ordered him to destroy that hope. Now Christ's passion also seemed to be the utter failure of what He had set out to do. When He was in the tomb, the Apostles dispersed, and the thing seemed hopeless. The passion and death of Christ were the supreme test of faith: from death came the Resurrection wherein the promise was fulfilled. And for us, too, it will often be only through the night of faith, through apparent failure, through the frustration of one hope after another, that God's plan for us will really be fulfilled in that mystery of death and resurrection which is at the very heart of the Christian life.

This is another of the elements always to be found in God's actions. And here again it is something so opposed to our human way of thinking that God, before showing it fully in Christ, willed to give men something that would prepare them for it. Otherwise the truth about Christ would have appeared so extraordinary, would have been such a shock to men's minds, that they could never really have been able to penetrate it. You may say that they were not able, even as it was. But this is for a different reason. And once again, as I shall show when I come to speak of her, for Our Lady at least the education was a success. That is why Our Lady consoles us for the others, consoles us for all the work of preparation wasted upon us.

The last of the *sacraments* I want to talk about is less

striking: it is the marriage of Isaac and Rebecca. The Fathers saw in it a figure of the marriage of the Word, first with the Jewish people, and later with all mankind; to them this marriage was the greatest of all mysteries— the fact that God has called us to some sort of sharing in His life, to an intercourse of which the figure is that between husband and wife. The Canticle of Canticles is not a love poem that found its way into the Bible by mistake; it is the very heart of the Bible, it is the marriage-song of the covenant between God and His people, between our soul and the Word. It is at once the great ecclesiological and cosmic poem of the marriage of mankind with the Word of God, and the inner poem singing the union of the Word with each soul, with all its changing pattern of infidelities and fidelities, which reaches its culmination in the perfect union we find in the great mystics.

The Fathers of the Church saw this already in figure with the patriarchs. Isaac, who was the son of the promise, and therefore a figure of Christ, married Rebecca, who had been found for him beside a well, which was, Origen tells us, a figure of the waters of baptism. Remember how the Epistle to the Ephesians says that the bridegroom must first cleanse the bride so as to present her holy and without blemish to God; that is to say, that, before He joins Himself to mankind, Christ must first wash them in the waters of baptism, that they may become wholly pure and holy, and able to celebrate their virginal marriage with Him.

When Isaac married the pagan Rebecca primitive mankind was betrothed; it was a far-off anticipation, a first mirroring of that marriage between the Church and Christ. Do not forget that here, too, there was a religious aspect, in that Isaac was imparting to Rebecca his faith, his worship of the one true God. Saint Ambrose explains the symbolism of the whole thing:

Rebecca came with the daughters of the city to draw water at the well, and because she came every day, Abraham's servant was able to find her, and she could marry Isaac. Do not think this is just a fable, or that the Holy Spirit is telling us stories in Scripture. It is a lesson to souls, and a spiritual doctrine to teach you to come to the Scriptures every day. All the things written in them are mysteries. Christ wishes to wed you, too. With this object He us sending you His servant— the word of the prophets. You will not be able to wed Christ unless you have first received His servant. Do not think it was by chance that so many patriarchs came to wells and were married by waters. The man who thinks that is like an animal, and cannot perceive the things that are of the spirit of God. Let him see no further than the things themselves if he wishes. But I tell you that they are figures, and the marriages of those holy men represent the union of the soul with the Word of God.

3. *The Blessing of Ismael*

To conclude with, a word about Ismael, whom we left beside our path, because the way to Christ did not pass through him. Ismael was the far-off ancestor of the Mahomedans, who have a special devotion to him. Mahomed says much more about him than about Isaac in the Koran. His story is most moving. He was the one God rejected in favour of the other, thus accomplishing the mystery of divine election. Ismael, however, was not without a certain protection from God. We read in Chapter xxi:

And when Sara had seen the son of Agar the Egyptian playing with Isaac her son, she said to Abraham: Cast out this bondwoman and her son; for the son of the bondwoman shall not be heir with my son Isaac. Abraham took this grievously for his son. And God said to him: Let not it seem grievous to thee . . . in Isaac shall thy seed be called. But I will make the son also of the bondwoman a great nation: because he is thy seed.

So Abraham rose up in the morning, and taking bread and a bottle of water, put it upon her shoulder, and delivered the boy, and sent her away. And she departed, and wandered in the wilderness of Bersabee. And when the water in the bottle was spent, she cast the boy under one of the trees that were there. And she went her way, and sat over against him. . . . And God heard the voice of the boy. And an angel of God called to Agar from heaven, saying: What art thou doing Agar? Fear not: for God hath heard the voice of the boy, from the place wherein he is. Arise, take up the boy, and hold him by the hand: for I will make him a great nation. And God opened her eyes; and she saw a well of water, and went and filled the bottle, and gave the boy to drink. And God was with him: and he grew, and dwelt in the wilderness, and became a young man, an archer.

It is a most moving passage, and shows us the tremendous mystery both of the divine election of souls and the divine election of peoples. Here we come right into the mystery of the Church's missionary work and the meaning of history. Saint Paul takes up this passage in the Epistle to the Galatians, and explains that here Agar is a figure of the Jewish people—which is a daring alteration of perspective: for the Jewish people were also a son, and were also rejected at a given moment to yield place to Abraham's sons according to the promise, the sons of Sara, the sons not of the bondwoman but of the free, who were, in fact, the Christians. You see, from this quotation of St. Paul, that there is indeed a mystery there, and a mystery accomplished twice over. The mystery whereby Isaac, father of the race of Israel, was chosen, and Ismael, father of the race of Arabs, the race of Mussulmans, was rejected—there is the first mystery of election and rejection. It may seem that in this there is something hard, something even tragic. Why choose one and not the other?

We find the same miracle again at the coming of Christ. There, too, we see a people rejected by God—the Jews— and another chosen—the Christian people, drawn from among the Gentiles. We find the same arrangement repeated. But this time we know that the cutting off of the Jews is only provisional, as Saint Paul tells us; that is to say, they are cut off "until the fulness of the Gentiles should come in", but when all the Gentiles have come in, then they, too, will come, and their return will be an even greater joy than the coming in of the Gentiles. (Rom. xi. 25–6).

I cannot but think there is a mystery of the same order prepared for the Mahomedans. Islam was also rejected, but we know it was not a rejection once and for all, that God's election is upon it, because it is of the race of Abraham according to the flesh, and God gave it His promises. Those promises may have been only of a temporal nature, but there was also a blessing which is still in force, and makes us wonder when the mystery will be accomplished, and when Ismael in his turn will come back—whether before or after the sons of Abraham—and rejoin the children of the promise.

This brings us to a further question: why one *before* the

other? and why one after the other? But that is the whole mystery of God's plan, in which we see successions and elections. Why was Christ born into the Jewish people? Why have we been Christians from the earliest days, whereas the people of China have not? It is the mystery of God's plan, and we can only adore His unfathomable ways; to do so calls for a depth of contemplation in us, of patience, of hope; but we do know that the mystery is that of universal salvation, of the salvation of the nations. In this plan of God's there is a place for the Jews, but there is also a place for Ismael, above that of the pagans, for Ismael has its own part in the mystery of history.

This realisation should give us a devotion to Abraham: indeed there is no point in speaking of him at all if it does not make us love him better; we should feel all the Old Testament characters closer to us, so that we really see them as saints interceding and praying for us. This has a special bearing on our missionary prayer, which we have long entrusted to Mary, to the angels, to all who did most to prepare the way of the Lord so mysteriously in the hearts of those who knew Him not. . . . Now Saint Abraham is the great intercessor for three very large categories of souls: for the Jews, because he was Isaac's father; for Islam, because he was Ismael's father; and, finally, for sinners, because it was he who besought God to save Sodom and Gomorrah —for those great sinners who are from time to time our spiritual responsibility, for those who are so deeply plunged in evil, and so far away from God, that they seem beyond hope. We may say of Abraham, that for all these he prays unwearyingly and without discouragement, and we learn from him to pray unwearyingly and without discouragement, too, for the Word of God changes hearts, and nothing is impossible to Him.

II

MELCHISEDECH AND THE COVENANT OF THE NATURAL UNIVERSE

WHEN Abraham answered God's call by leaving Haran, and arrived in Chanaan, thus inaugurating sacred history, he was greeted by a mysterious person, of whom all we know is contained in two verses of Genesis: "But Melchisedech, the king of Salem, bringing forth bread and wine, for he was the priest of the most high God, blessed him, and said: Blessed be Abram by the most high God, who created heaven and earth" (Gen. xiv. 18–19). Everything about this text is mysterious. The text itself belongs to some totally different document, and its being in the Bible at all is an enigma to the exegetes. The author of the Epistle to the Hebrews points out with what mystery it is surrounded: "For this Melchisedech was king of Salem, priest of the most high God, who met Abraham returning from the slaughter of the kings, and blessed him: to whom also Abraham divided the tithes of all: who first indeed by interpretation is king of justice: and then also king of Salem, that is king of peace: without father, without mother, without genealogy, having neither beginning of days nor end of life" (Heb. vii. 1–3).

Now the whole thought of the Bible invests this mysterious personage with great importance. Psalm cix sees in his priesthood a figure of the priesthood of the Messias: *Tu es sacerdos in aeternum secundum ordinem Melchisedech.*[1]

[1] See G. Bardy, *Melchisédech dans la tradition patristique*; *Rev. Bibl.*, 1926, pp. 416 ff.; 1927, pp. 24 ff.

In the New Testament he has a tremendous significance. The author of the Epistle to the Hebrews writes that he "continueth a priest forever" (vii. 3). And it furthermore places his priesthood above the Levitical priesthood, because the latter was only a provisional one, to be made void by the coming of Christ, whereas Melchisedech's priesthood is eternal. "If then perfection was by the Levitical priesthood (for under it the people received the law), what further need was there that another priest should rise according to the order of Melchisedech: and not be called according to the order of Aaron?" (Heb. vii. 11). This priesthood of Melchisedech's was to prefigure the priesthood of Christ, the true High Priest— "the forerunner Jesus is entered for us, made a high priest forever according to the order of Melchisedech" (vi. 20). This is so, in that Melchisedech's priesthood is made "not according to the law of a carnal commandment, but according to the power of an indissoluble life" (vii. 16). That is why he was "likened unto the Son of God" (vii. 3). He is greater even than Abraham. "Now consider how great this man is, to whom also Abraham the patriarch gave tithes out of the principal things. . . . And he . . . blessed him that had the promises. And without all contradiction, that which is less is blessed by the better" (vii. 4, 6, 7). The Fathers of the Church even go so far as to see him not as a historical personage, but an appearance of the Word, or the Holy Spirit. Thus Saint Ambrose writes: "Who is Melchisedech, whose name means King of Justice? Can an ordinary man be the king of justice? He can be none other than the Wisdom of God."[1]

Who in fact was this mysterious person? We have no cause to doubt what the Bible has to tell us about him. "It is not impossible," writes M. Lods,[2] "that, as a Jewish

[1] P. L. xiv. 438 B.   [2] *Israël des origines au milieu du VIIIe siècle*, p. 164.

midrash preserved in Genesis has it, there was a city in Chanaan which gave its God the title El Elyon (Most High God), creator of heaven and earth. The Phoenicians also had two divinities, one called El, the other Elioun." The city of Salem of which Melchisedech was king, is thought to have been near Jerusalem, and, in any case, may well have been a city of Chanaan before the days of the Israelites. The fact of Melchisedech's being at once king and priest would fit in very well with an archaic time when the function of priest was exercised by the head of the family or tribe, and there was as yet no specialised priesthood as such. This seems to have been particularly true of ancient Chanaan. "The existence of priests," writes M. Lods[1] "is not found explicitly attested by monuments so far discovered." And he quotes a text from an Egyptian who journeyed into Palestine around 1117 and saw there a king offering sacrifice. It is only very lately that archæological discoveries in Chanaan have come to confirm most astoundingly even this matter of offerings to the gods not only of bloody sacrifices but also of bread and wine. M. Lods goes on: "They made libations, for a lot of cups have been found that were used for the purpose. They also brought them vegetable offerings, particularly loaves or cakes, which could, if need be, be replaced by baked rolls of earth, made in the same shape. Hundreds such have been found in the sanctuaries of Beisân".[2] Thus the king of Salem emerges from the mystery the Epistle to the Hebrews surrounds him with. He appears in his historical context as a king-priest of ancient Chanaan who welcomed Abraham upon his arrival in the land of promise, by presenting the offerings of his religion.

[1] *Op. cit.*, p. 117.
[2] *Op. cit.*, p. 115.

But at the same time his significance and his importance grow much clearer to us. What in fact was this religion of ancient Chanaan, which existed before the true religion inaugurated by Abraham? It was the religion of the natural universe, the first religion of mankind, corresponding to the first revelation. By first revelation I do not mean a primitive revelation, made to the first men and handed down by tradition. There is nothing to justify such traditionalism; the literary genre of the narratives at the beginning of Genesis means that Scripture does not bind us in the matter, and the facts do not support it. I am referring to God's revelation through nature, which corresponds to the first covenant, the covenant with Noe, by which God bound Himself to observe the laws of the seasons, to make them rainy and dry at the proper times, so that man should get to know His personal Providence by the fidelity with which He gave His gifts. This covenant is related in the Book of Genesis, after the story of the Flood (ix. 8–12). The rainbow was the evidence of this covenant, just as the paschal lamb was of the Mosaic covenant. There are two most important texts in the New Testament to remind us that this was indeed an authentic revelation of God, as Providence, addressed to all men: " . . . the living God, who made the heaven and the earth and the sea and all things that are in them: who in times past suffered all nations to walk in their own ways. Nevertheless he left not himself without testimony, doing good from heaven, giving rains and fruitful seasons, filling our hearts with food and gladness" (Acts xiv. 14–16). These words were said by Saint Paul to the pagans of Lystra. And it was also pagans to whom he referred when he wrote in the Epistle to the Romans: "For the invisible things of him from the creation of the world are clearly seen, being understood by the things

that are made. His eternal power also and divinity"
(Rom. i. 20).

This primitive religion had been deformed, profaned,
perverted by the different sorts of idolatry: "and they
changed the glory of the incorruptible God into the
likeness of the image of a corruptible man and of
birds, and of fourfooted beasts and of creeping things"
(Rom. i. 23).

We cannot but recall here the Chananean worship
of the bird of Astarte[1] and the warning against wor-
shipping the serpent, symbol of fertility, which is in the
background of the story of the Fall in Genesis.[2] But beneath
all these perversions, that first religion nevertheless continued. "It is still for us the most sacred mystery in its
most elementary form—the obscure intuition that God is
somehow present in the silence of the night, the darkness of
the forest, the immensity of the desert, the fire of genius,
the purity of love."[3] And Melchisedech seems to rise out
of the yet unspoiled depth of this primitive religion, still
bathed in the innocence of Eden. Among all the cults of
Chanaan, even then perverted, cruel and immoral as they
were, he appears as the one priest faithful to the covenant
of Noe, as if preserved by a miracle from the impurities
which began to fill the earth again as soon as the Flood was
over, so that when Abraham came on the scene he could
give him the greeting of primitive religion. He was the
priest of God "who created heaven and earth", the
God of creation of whom Saint Paul tells us in the Acts
that He did not leave Himself without testimony. And
Père Féret, in a most remarkable study of Melchisedech,
remarks that "this bread and wine which he presented to

[1] Lods, *op. cit.*, p. 90.
[2] Paul Humbert, *Études sur le récit du Paradis et de la Chute dans la Genèse*,
Neufchâtel, 1940, p. 75.
[3] *Le Signe du Temple*, p. 10.

Abraham, as a gesture of hospitality that was at once religious and charitable, were a more spiritual offering, and nearer to the simplicity of nature, than all the sacred slaying of animals prescribed in the Mosaic law".[1]

For though the covenant with Abraham marks a further stage, and an advance in God's plan, it is also, under certain aspects, apparently, a step backwards. Melchisedech's religion covered all mankind. It was a covenant made with "all nations" (Acts xiv. 15). The covenant with Abraham, on the other hand, concerned only one people. It was a narrowing down, though of course, only for a time, whereby for nineteen hundred years the nations would be left out of the New Covenant. Melchisedech's priesthood was the sacrifice of all mankind, for man is the priest of creation. It was not the privilege of a special caste. "Melchisedech," wrote Eusebius, "was not chosen by men, nor anointed with man-made oils ".[2] In Israel, on the contrary, the highest act of worship was to be the prerogative of a particular tribe, the tribe of Levi, and the rest were to be excluded. Melchisedech's sacrifice could be offered anywhere, by anyone. It was not limited to one special place. Henceforth worship was to become more and more localised to a single spot. "Destroy all the places in which the nations that you shall possess, worshipped their gods upon high mountains, and hills, and under every shady tree" (Deut. xii. 2). It is the ancient cult of Chanaan, of Melchisedech, that is here forbidden. It is then clear that in many ways Christian worship is more like that of Melchisedech than that of the Levites. And this gives us an inkling as to why Paul placed Melchisedech above Abraham. He was indeed the figure, similar though imperfect, of Him who was to be "high priest according to the

[1] *La messe et sa catéchèse, Lex orandi*, 1947, p. 229.
[2] *Demonstr. Evang.*, v.

order of Melchisedech ". But the narrowing down effected by the covenant with Abraham was absolutely necessary: "By separating man from God, it made clear two things. It showed first the grandeur and holiness of God: we see what degraded gods the Greeks came to believe in, as a result of too much familiarity, of anthropomorphism. . . . It pointed next to the sinfulness of man, and developed his sense of that fundamental lack of purity which we call original sin. It made him in this way realise his utter poverty, and hope for a liberator ".[1] In God's mysterious plan this was a fresh beginning, a new value acquired.

It is from this that the meeting between Melchisedech and Abraham takes all its significance. When Abraham appeared to inaugurate a new order of things, which was to supplant theirs and make it void, the representatives of the religion of the natural universe could have reacted in one of two ways. They could have clung to the revelation they already had, which was a true revelation from God, and refused to recognise this man whom God was sending to set up a new religion to supplant theirs. That was how the pagan world as a whole behaved. That is how the pagan world is behaving today in refusing to recognise the true religion. That was the attitude later adopted by the Jewish people when the third stage in God's plan came to pass. That is *the tragedy of the forerunners*. A forerunner is a man sent by God to lay down the road for someone else. When that someone himself appears, then the forerunner's mission is done and he must give way. To do that is heroic—it means being content to join the rank and file, to become a disciple after being a master. And there is an enormous temptation to refuse to humble oneself. Thus the pagans refused to recognise God's revelation to Abraham. And they still refuse. Thus the Jewish people

[1] *Le Signe du Temple*, p. 18.

refuse to recognise Our Lord. In a very fine passage from his book, *Der Herr*, Guardini says that Buddha was one of Christ's greatest forerunners, and will be the last adversary to yield to Him. Buddha, a lofty representative of the religion of the natural universe, the pre-Biblical religion, was the one who by forming its soul, prepared India most mysteriously in the far past to receive Jesus Christ, but he, too, in the last great drama of the world, when even Israel "shall be grafted in" (Rom. xi. 23), will be the one to fight Christ for the soul of India, by setting against the universalism of Christianity, the universalism of the religion of the natural universe, which is the thing that most resembles it, the caricature of catholicity, syncretism. So the forerunner can become the opponent.

That is not the only reaction possible. The forerunner *may* receive with joy the one for whom it was his work to prepare, and "rejoice when he hears the bridegroom's voice". This is where we see the real significance of Melchisedech's meeting with Abraham. In Melchisedech the religion of the natural universe came for the first time, by the guidance of the Holy Spirit, to greet the religion of the Bible at its start and do homage to it. The tradition of the one covenant *had* to be handed on to the other, and Melchisedech, coming forward from the mysterious depths of the covenant with Noe, "without father, without mother", comments Saint Paul, because he did not stand for any particular race, but for all mankind, was the representative of that first covenant. We cannot help being reminded of another meeting, where Abraham's religion, in turn, was to greet Christ's at its start; at about the same place where the first meeting happened. John the Baptist, the greatest of the prophets, representing the whole of the Old Testament, was in its name to greet Jesus, whom God manifested to him by the Jordan as the inaugurator of the third Covenant; he proclaimed: "This is he who was to come", and then faded out of the picture himself. Thus, at the changing-places of the covenants, we find Melchisedech and John—one rising up from the paradisal world which was to all appearances buried in idolatry, and the other rekindling the flame of a prophecy long extinguished under the ashes of legalism; each with the mission of bringing salutation in God's name from the religion of the past to the founder of the religion of the future.

But one further note must be added. When Abraham's covenant came to supplant that of Noe it did not mean the substitution of some totally new religion for the old, so that the first was completely to disappear, any more than it did when Christ's Covenant came to supplant Abraham's. On the contrary, it involved a succession in which the new order, far from dethroning the old, fulfilled it, and included it while transcending it. It is like the growth of a man, in which the passing from childhood into youth and from youth into maturity are fruitful turning-points in which all the riches of the earlier stage are taken up in the greater harmony of the later. Thus with Christ, who "came not to destroy but to fulfil" the old covenant. Similarly, the old covenant had not destroyed, but fulfilled, the covenant of the natural universe. Indeed, history tells us so. When, after the captivity in Egypt, Abraham's descendants entered into possession of the land of Melchisedech, that land of Chanaan which their ancestor had passed through five hundred years before them, they fitted their faith, their monotheism, into the old religious forms of Chanaan. Or, more precisely speaking their attitude was twofold, as is always the case on such occasions, as was the case with Christianity in regard to the paganism it met in its early days.

On the one hand, the prophets were always having to warn them against the content of the old worship, and condemn the old rites; but at the same time they borrowed certain elements from these forms of worship, while substituting their religion for the worship itself. Thus the story of the sacrificing of Isaac is in part a warning against the Chananean (or Phoenician) custom of child sacrifice, and the story in Genesis a warning against the adoration of the serpent. But we see the brazen serpent coming in later as a sacrament of the worship of God, and Christ Himself saw in that a figure of His own lifting up on the cross. We also see the first-born of the flock substituted for the first-born of the family as the victim of sacrifice, though the same meaning attached to them. And they also were to be a figure of the sacrifice consummated in the fulness of time by "the first-born among the dead". The Temple was to retain a clear cosmic significance, representing with its three courts sky, earth and sea.[1] And Carmel, the holy place of the Chanaanites, was to remain the home of prophetic inspiration until it became the mystical summit of the soul's ascent in the divine night of Saint John of the Cross.

Judaism took this cosmic religion to itself, and Christianity does the same. And, as the everlasting symbol of this assumption, we come back once more to the Eucharist. When Christ, at the Last Supper, took bread and wine to make them the visible matter of the Eucharist, it is more than likely that He meant to recall the occasion when Melchisedech also offered bread and wine. Père Féret writes: "Try to make real to yourself the Last Supper, from the Scriptural account in all its implications—as it was actually happening, and in its power of bringing to mind all the rest of the Bible—and then what the Epistle to the

---

[1] *Le Signe du Temple*, p. 19.

Hebrews has to say about Christ's priesthood according to the order of Melchisedech will not seem unwarranted; it is firmly based on what happened in the Gospels, particularly on the offering of bread and wine ".[1]

Just as Christ, instituting the Blessed Sacrament in the course of the Paschal meal, showed that there was a continuity between it and the Mosaic covenant, so by instituting it under the appearances of bread and wine He showed its continuity with the covenant made with Noe, whose high priest was Melchisedech. Christ, then, was not only carrying out the Old Testament worship and giving reality to what was there in figure, but in His own sacrifice He was taking up all together and, as it were, giving a new reality to all the sacrifices men had offered in all religions, at all times. All the efforts ever made to worship God and enter into communion with Him, which had never been fully able to achieve their end, were thus completed and perfected in Christ's sacrifice. And this is symbolised by the use of bread and wine, which showed that Abraham's religion, restricted to the Jewish people, was only a stage, and that in Christ all mankind gives glory to God and enters into communion with Him. That is why the liturgy of the Mass, after speaking of the "sacrifice of our father Abraham", immediately goes on to add that offered by *summus sacerdos Melchisedech, sanctum sacrificium, immaculatam hostiam.*

And this again raises the problem of Christianity's relation to the non-Christian religions: in the strictest sense of the word a *missionary* problem. After all, the sacramental gestures in all religions are so alike that many people today find it most difficult to see in what Christianity is any different from the others, and wherein it transcends them. Sacramentalism is, in fact, the point at which

[1] *op. cit.,* p. 229.

Christianity is most deeply bound up with all the religions of the world. And while this presents a great difficulty to some, it is, from our point of view, tremendously important. To certain minds the difficulty is enormous. It involves the whole history of comparative religions. My reason for attempting to grapple with it is that it is one of the points we are most questioned about nowadays. We find so many people who think that as long as you have *some* religion, it does not matter which, and cannot see why, if men are finding God through Buddhism or Hinduism, you should want to impose on them the Christian religion which seems so much a thing of the West, unsuited to other continents.

We know a man can be saved in *any* religion—and yet our one wish is that everyone be converted to Christianity. This is likely to put us in rather a difficult position, but we must not try to slide out of the difficulty where truth is involved. This is the paradoxical position our theology places us in. It was far easier for the Jansenists to say: Everyone not baptised goes to hell. But we know that we have no right to say that. We must not say a thing because it is the easiest thing to say. We must learn to stick to the truth even when the truth is harder. Therefore we must say both that you can be saved outside Christianity—not outside Christ, of course, but there are all sorts of mysterious ways in which men belong to Christ and are saved—and yet that it is still necessary that all men become Christians and converts to the faith of Christ

This problem presents itself in a special way on the sacramental plane. For here, the similarity between Christianity and the other religions is quite extraordinary. Take baptism, for instance. Anyone who has given a little study to the history of different religions will tell you that baptisms are found everywhere, that the ceremony is universal. About the time of Christ there were Jewish sects who practised it—so much so that some writers have thought Christianity simply a development of one of these. Look at the pagan mysteries in the ancient world, the Eleusinian mysteries which were the most advanced of the religious forms existing at the time of Christ. On the second day of purification they were made to go into the sea for the bath of purification, before being initiated further into the mysteries. We are told, therefore, that there was nothing original in Christian baptism: people were used to finding this sort of thing in all the mysteries, and Christianity was just one mystery with the same elements as all the others—baptism, the purifying bath, the initiation and revealing of secret doctrines, the sacred meal as a symbol of unity.

And it is true there is a great resemblance. Take the modern world. Remember all the religious immersions in the Ganges. One cannot help thinking that just as the Jordan was once the river laden with grace so the Ganges might become a river of grace, a holy river, an image of the Holy Spirit, so that the people who bathe in it would be not merely seeking an external purification, but could draw from it birth into new life. God grant that the waters of the Ganges may become the waters of baptism, and the Ganges a new Jordan. For is there not in this bathing in the Ganges something which is a sort of expectation, a sort of anticipation of what may one day be the baptising of India? This awakens the deepest echoes in us, for it is one of those profound analogies whose significance is full of mystery, which we would do well to study.

I took baptism as my example, but I could just as easily take any of the others; for instance, the sacred meal, signifying to us communion with God—to them communion with a god. This is also a ceremony we find in all religions: there is a sacrifice, whereby a living being is consecrated to the god, followed by a sharing out of the victim, which signifies a communion of life between the god and the worshippers. Once again a form of worship used in all religions. There are many such examples which may be quoted. I shall come back to this, for we must get to the bottom of all these problems by studying and meditating on them.

There is one aspect of this which can prove disturbing. We are asked: But then what is the difference between Christianity and the other religions? To us this should be a thing which, far from being disturbing, is extremely interesting. What are these rites which we find cropping up in all religions? They are there for just this reason: that in every religion there is an obscure intuition that material actions are full of mystery, and the visible elements and all material things are ways by which we come to God. Men need to be purified. What more natural action to express purification from sin than pouring water which cleanses? What more natural to express communion with God than a meal, in which you share the same bread, and in which this same bread in each one's body signifies a sort of shared life? Here, too, how could people fail to see in this rite an expression of the idea of communion with God?

Therefore, what we find here is simply that species of universal sacramentalism which is a sort of deep intuition of the divine meaning of things, and which signifies grace, though it does not effect what it signifies. It is a sort of foreshadowing, a sort of call. . . . What is Christianity to do? Should it create new rites, quite different from those in other religions? Not at all. Christianity was to adopt those sacred actions of all religions, now shot through with the grace of Christ. Thus, this water of the Ganges, inasmuch as it becomes baptism, becomes the means of supernatural birth for men. The meal, too, remains the same, but the bread to be broken is not simply a symbol, for now it makes us in fact communicate with the very reality of Jesus Christ.

You see, then, what is the same and what is not. It is almost exactly the same, and it is utterly different. It is the same insofar as the gesture is concerned, but different because the figure is not the reality, the gesture of expectation is not the gift. A gift—there you have the essence of Christianity: God's gift of divine grace and divine life. You see why this interests us so much: we see sacramentalism as essentially the way in which Christianity is incarnated in the religions of the world, that is to say, the way in which Christianity carries them further without destroying them, by making use of all in them that is good, all that prepares them for it, all these religious gestures. That was what Christ was doing when He did the thing Melchisedech had done. That is how we come to speak of these other religions as a sort of prefiguring, of preparation for Christ. We are always on the lookout for signs that this is so. And we delight to recognise in all the great civilisations their particular foreshadowing for each of our sacraments.

PART II
THE LAST PRECURSORS

I

JOHN THE BAPTIST

WE HAVE noted in this brief study of the Old Testament how God—for His work upon us is always done in time, and His plans therefore unfold over a long course of years —made the earth ready for Christ's coming, and we mentioned a few of those who prepared the way of the Lord. Saint John the Baptist came on the scene at the end of this long preparation, the last to arrive before the Lord Himself, whom he greeted in the name of all mankind. The others had all told men about the Lord who was to come: he showed the Jews Our Lord present among them, saying: "Behold the Lamb of God . . ." *Ecce!*[1]

In studying John the Baptist, the first thing that strikes us is the way in which God marked him out for Himself. In this, John the Baptist is the model for all those who are called to devote themselves wholly to preparing God's ways. He was marked out by God, and his life was eminently a consecrated one: it was so even before he was born. He is in a class of humanity by himself, lower than Our Lady, of course, who is above all other creatures, yet different from the other saints, for he was sanctified even in the womb of his mother during that most mysterious episode, the Visitation. At that moment Jesus, alive in Mary, sanctified John the Baptist; and John, before his birth, leaped in his mother's womb, filled with the Holy

[1] André Retif made a study of the missionary theology of the Precursor in *Jean le Baptiste, missionaire du Christ*, "La Sphère et la Croix", Editions du Seuil, 1948.

Spirit who was thus communicated to him, and who had already sanctified him. This seems to have been a fulfilment, even as early as this, of what John was later to say: that he rejoiced "with joy because of the bridegroom's voice". He leapt for joy on that day, when, alive in his mother's womb, he heard Mary greeting Elizabeth. There seems to have been some strange affinity between him and Our Lord, whereby he could not help thrilling to Our Lord's presence. He was the man who gave up all other joys for the joy of hearing his Lord's voice.

That is why he appears to us cut off from all created things, a man set apart for this one great joy. He wanted no other joys; he wanted no other consolation. That joy was the one thing he lived for. And it was that joy that overwhelmed him even before he was born. He was henceforward to live only for this. He was to have, as Father Faber remarked, "a blessed inability to attach himself to the things of earth". He was so filled by the Holy Spirit that he became somehow unable to live by anything else. He knew what true joy was, and so could know no other—this is the meaning of his life in the desert.

Saint Luke notes in his Gospel, after the Visitation: "And the child grew and was strengthened in spirit"— always *in spirit*—"and was in the deserts until the day of his manifestation to Israel." We know something of his life—the joy of his first meeting with Christ, when, before he was even born, he played his part of forerunner, and then the joy of the second meeting, Christ's baptism, when the friend of the bridegroom "rejoiced with joy because of the bridegroom's voice"; but between these two meetings there was a long time spent in the desert, spent, that is, where there was naught to speak to him save God. It was in the desert that Psichari got back his sense of God's presence, for there God is nearer, and there we are least distracted from Him by His creatures. . . . It was there that the men we now call Desert Fathers buried themselves in the fourth century. This was an extraordinary thing to happen at that time in the history of the Church. Antony, an Egyptian living in the suburbs of Alexandria, was the first of many to take refuge in the desert, so as to be more completely alone with God, to carry on the spiritual struggle at its fiercest—for while the desert is where God's presence is most felt, it is also where Christ was tempted, and where Antony was tempted, and where, far from the wars of men, the spiritual battle between Christ and Satan for the souls of men becomes most intense. John the Baptist was the first thus to fly to the desert for solitude—before Christ, before Antony, before all the rest—to concentrate all his energies on the spiritual struggle, so as not to be drawn aside from it by anything which would not serve to prepare for the Kingdom of God by victories of Love.

But he is the saint of the desert only because he is the saint of spiritual joy. In the collect for the feast of John the Baptist we ask him for the grace of spiritual joy, the grace that was most specially his. He is the most jubilant saint of all Scripture. But he is a "one-joy man", and his joy was to hear the voice of his Lord. He escaped into the desert so that nothing could turn him from that joy, so that he could give himself entirely to it, so that he could be always meditating upon the first meeting before he was born, and awaiting the second meeting, Our Lord's baptism, keeping apart from all other creatures to prepare himself for that unique joy.

The striking thing about John the Baptist is the mixture in him of a tremendous spirit of penance, and inner jubilation, the union of great penance with great joy.

However, there is a link between great penance and deep joy; the greatest penitents have always been the loudest in rejoicing. There is no joy greater than the joy of Francis of Assisi, of John of the Cross, of the Curé of Ars, of the Fathers of the Egyptian desert.

As John announced Christ even before his birth, so he was the forerunner of His public life. Now, after the desert, came the culminating moment of his life, while he was preparing the way of Christ: "There was a man sent from God whose name was John. This man came for a witness to give testimony of the Light, that all men might believe through him. He was not the Light, but was to give testimony of the Light." John the Baptist's essential work, then, was to give testimony of the Light, to show Christ. He had a most important part to play in the preparation for Christ's coming, and Christ's work itself. He it was who laid the ground for Our Lord's public life, and for His teaching, by making men's souls ready for it. He was to some extent educating souls, taking the first steps towards laying them more open to receive what Christ was to tell them. Christ's words would have been too much for souls not prepared for them. They had to have some previous education. Their interests had to be given a new twist away from their earthly concerns and customs, they must be made to feel that all was not well.

That was John the Baptist's task. Among men totally unconcerned with the things of God, it was his work to awaken their interest, unsettle them from their complacency and arouse in them enough good will to understand Christ when He came.

In this he was in the same position as all who had earlier shared in the work of preparing for the Lord's coming; they, too, were separated from earthly things by

God, and mysteriously given to see His plans, so that they might trace His ways to men. Saint John came in his turn to trace His ways to men, to make the rough ways plain, to bring the mountains low. But in order to do this he must first be completely caught up by his inward vision, he must belong to the Lord utterly, for the ground he had to break was hard: he was coming amongst the men of his day, who were mainly engaged, like those of our own, as Saint Luke tells us, the soldiers in doing violence and spreading calumny, the publicans in taking more than their due (iii. 11–14).

Human beings are like that—they were then, and they are now. They are busy about earthly affairs. They are completely heedless of God, and our chief feeling as we move among them is one of anguish at seeing the world's utter indifference to anything higher.

To shake the world out of this indifference we need prophets, that is to say, men whose souls are captured by the divine vision of things and who can shake the mass of men out of their inertia, and be, in truth, "witnesses". Now a witness is someone to whom it is granted to see things as God does, and who has this inner vision himself in such a way that he can hand it on to mankind. Such a man was John the Baptist. God first let him into the mystery of His design, then drew him apart into the desert to unite him to His own joy. And then—and this is the important part—he became a "witness"—that is, one who shows men Christ.

In Saint Matthew's Gospel, chapter iii, John the Baptist appears to us like this:

> And in those days cometh John the Baptist, preaching in the desert of Judea, and saying: Do penance, for the kingdom of heaven is at hand. For this is he that was

spoken of by Isaias the prophet saying: A voice of one
crying in the desert, Prepare ye the way of the Lord,
make straight his paths.

It is interesting to compare this with the original text.
Here is the passage from Isaias referred to by John the
Baptist:

> Be comforted, be comforted, my people, saith your
> God. Speak ye to the heart of Jerusalem, and call to
> her: for her evil is come to an end, her iniquity is
> forgiven: she hath received of the hand of the Lord
> double for all her sins. The voice of one crying in the
> desert: Prepare ye the way of the Lord, make straight
> in the wilderness the paths of our God. Every valley
> shall be exalted, and every mountain and hill shall be
> made low, and the crooked shall become straight
> and the rough ways plain. And the glory of the Lord
> shall be revealed, and all flesh together shall see,
> that the mouth of the Lord hath spoken (Isa. xl.
> 1–5).

What he was referring to, then, was Iahweh coming in
glory, and the resurrection of mankind. That is what John
the Baptist was announcing when he besought men to get
themselves ready by doing penance; that is what was
imminent at the start of the Gospels. That is why we
observe so much more violence and intensity than anything to be found in the Old Testament. The thing was
now actually about to happen: the glory of God was to
appear, and mankind was to find itself face to face with
that glory. No more time must be lost, it was not the
moment for each to go his own way, but for all to prepare
for the Lord's coming by penance.

John the Baptist puts this very strongly when he is talk-
ing to the Pharisees: "Ye brood of vipers, who hath shewed
you to flee from the wrath to come? . . . For now the axe
is laid to the root of the trees." So the ancient tree is
about to fall. "Every tree therefore that doth not yield
good fruit, shall be cut down and cast into the fire. I
indeed baptise you in water unto penance, but he that
shall come after me is mightier than I, whose shoes I am
not worthy to bear; he shall baptise you in the Holy
Ghost and fire." The Holy Ghost and fire here have an
eschatological significance. The fire is the fire of judgment, which is at the same time the fire of Love. It is the
very glory of God that will transform the just, and destroy
sin. John the Baptist's baptism of water was only a figure
and a preparation for this. Not till the fire and the Holy
Ghost appear will the transfiguring and transforming
of the world which Christ is going to accomplish be
complete.

John the Baptist is, then, announcing the coming of the
King and Judge, the "parousia" of Christ in glory, but
he is also announcing the coming of the Bridegroom,
another name for "Him that is to come". He that is to
come is the Lord of Glory who will judge the living and
the dead, but He is also the Bridegroom spoken of by the
Canticle of Canticles and the Prophets, coming to meet
mankind whom He has chosen, to unite them to Himself
in one flesh—His flesh—so as to bring them into His
Father's House.

And this was to be not a call to fear and penance before
God's all-devouring fire, but, on the contrary, a call to joy.
It was a call to joy because the time had come for the long-
awaited marriage of humanity, when it was to be truly
united to the Word of God. And John was the friend of
the Bridegroom, that is to say that, as was the custom in

weddings of old, he was the one who brought him his betrothed. You know the text: "A man cannot receive anything unless it be given him from heaven. You yourselves do bear me witness, that I said, I am not Christ, but that I am sent before him. He that hath the bride is the bridegroom: but the friend of the bridegroom, who standeth and heareth him, rejoiceth with joy because of the bridegroom's voice. This my joy therefore is fulfilled. He must increase, but I must decrease." This is the sentence that throws the greatest light on John the Baptist's character. He "rejoiceth with joy because of the bridegroom's voice". He was the one to hear the Bridegroom's voice, the voice that Abraham had not heard, that Moses had not heard, that David had not heard. But John the Baptist heard it. It was in him that mankind met the Bridegroom; it was he who went before Him, and who, therefore, was present at the dawn of His marriage, celebrated in the Incarnation, and consummated in the Passion and Resurrection.

That is why we find the terrific violence of John the Baptist coupled with great gentleness. He was at once the fiercest and sweetest of men. He was the most violent because he really *realised* the Holiness of God, and had, therefore, a tremendous sense of sin and of penance; he stands out as *the* saint of purification. And he is at the same time a saint of great joy, of great gentleness. But in fact the two things are most closely linked. In the lives of the great mystics, we find that spiritual marriage and the absolute summit of Union are neighboured with the most painful and far-reaching purification. It looks as if at the very moment of being thus united to the Word humanity must be made to feel more deeply than ever how it needs this purification of fire, and that only the fire of the Spirit can make it fit for its wedding.

And John the Baptist had the great joy of knowing that his testimony was heard, as those who had been his disciples recognised Christ. He had prepared the way, and now John, Peter, James, the disciples he had prepared, recognised Christ when He came. John showed Him to them as the Lamb of God. And there lay John's great joy —the joy of seeing the bride meeting the Bridegroom. That was all he wanted. His one wish was to lead souls to Christ, take them to meet Him. At that moment of meeting his joy was complete. When his disciples left him to follow Christ it was perfect. He wanted nothing else. It was he who had come to prepare the way of the Lord. He had no wish to keep any souls for himself. In this he is the perfect model of self-denial. He never wanted anyone to grow attached to him—his one wish was to attach everyone to Christ. Having once prepared the way, he then faded out himself to leave them with the Bridegroom, with Christ.

And there you have the chief thing we must keep in mind concerning him: he was the man whose love expressed itself in disinterested zeal—that is to say, we see it less from his delight in Christ's personal presence, for after all from this he was often separated, than from his perfect fidelity in carrying out the mission he had been given, and thus leading souls to Christ. It is this that gives his love its special character. It consisted chiefly in wanting Christ to feel the joy of having souls, of finding more and more souls brought to Him. It was for this that Christ thirsted. It was this that John worked for. He took more delight in giving Christ joy than in himself enjoying Christ—if I may put it so. This means that there must have been some most special grace of love given him. He was indeed the servant whose love was, above all, expressed by serving, doing whatever Christ wanted, whatever Christ commanded. Serving perfectly. Our Lord wants His servants to be like that. "I have found a man after my own heart, who does all that I ask of him," as we read in a verse of a psalm. There are so few men Christ can make free with. The souls He loves most are those He can make free with, those of whom He can ask whatever He wants, souls which are His to dispose of. Now John the Baptist was, above all, a man who put himself completely into Our Lord's hands, the perfect servant who did what his master wanted, whose joy was to hear the Bridegroom's voice.

That was not John the Baptist's only work; he was not here only to prepare souls for Christ. He had also a special function to fulfil in regard to Christ Himself, for it was he who was mysteriously called on to baptise Christ, though Christ had no need of baptism. Christ did not need it, but His action shows us His tremendous humility in taking upon Himself the sin of mankind, in putting Himself in the position of those who did need baptism. And the Father answered this humility by that tremendous manifestation of the Trinity, when He said: "This is my beloved son", and the Holy Ghost also descended upon Him. Saint John the Baptist was therefore the instrument by which Christ was first shown to us for what He was— the Son of God. He revealed the Mystery of the Trinity to John, and it was through John that the mystery was shown to us at the start of Jesus' career, through him that Jesus' ministry was established. He went before Christ like a herald up to the beginning of the public life.

Thus did God form John, cutting him off from the things of earth, bringing him into His own secrets. Once prepared, he was the instrument for preparing other souls to receive Christ. And then, what is so mysterious and so moving in his life, his work done, he fell back into obscurity.

He was rejected; he disappeared; he drew aside. Once Christ had come there was nothing more for him to do. "He must increase, and I must decrease." The end of his life seemed to be forlorn, stripped bare, abandoned. Having had his share in the mystery of Christ's preaching, he was now sharing in His Passion.[1] Péguy remarks of Joan of Arc that her imitation of Christ was perfect in that, having taken part in His struggle, she, too, ended life in failure, forgotten, rejected, abandoned, forlorn. Many saints have longed that, their usefulness once over, they might have such an end.

In the life of John the Baptist the end is truly strange and overwhelming. We first see how utterly he was abandoned by his followers. His disciples lost interest in him. Christ was there; John did not matter any more. John the Baptist, who was a great prophet, who drew immense crowds by the Jordan, was now left without a single follower. All his former disciples now followed Christ, and indeed were right to do so. He was quite content to be thus left; he looked at Christ and the disciples from a distance. He did not even have the joy of living among them, living with Christ. We might have expected that! But no, he left that joy to others. He did what he was sent to do and no more. That done, he stepped aside.

He was not only abandoned by others, but—and this bears on some of the most mysterious things about the end of his life—one has a feeling almost as though he had been abandoned by God, rather as Our Lord was on the cross. In that strange episode when he sent his disciples to Jesus to ask whether He was really He that was to come it is as if there was for that moment a clouding over—the last

[1] L. Zander deals with this very well in *Le Précurseur selon le Père Boulghakov, Dieu vivant,* vii, 107 ff.

purification by which God was preparing him to be fully united to Himself—a moment in which, humanly, he lost all clarity of vision, held on only to the purity and self-denial of his life, went through the hardest tests of faith, which God lets His greatest friends go through that their faith may be well and truly tried.

And at the end of it all John gave Love's supreme testimony; he was imprisoned and then killed because he went on giving witness to the truth to the very end. He was imprisoned, beheaded, abandoned, forgotten; he had given up everything down to life itself. Here we touch on something very mysterious: there was a brief time when he appeared as a great prophet preparing men to hear the Lord's voice, and on either side two abysses of obscurity—the desert at the beginning, and prison at the end; therefore, during that brief time his essential characteristic was seen in all its fulness—he was wholly and solely the voice of one crying in the wilderness; his whole life, then, seems somehow to have been concentrated into that brief space when he was the voice witnessing to Christ, and for the rest he lived in obscurity and expectation.

We find displayed in John the Baptist's life various main characteristics which ought to attach to all whose work is to prepare the way of the Lord. What is certain is that John is still carrying on this work of his in the Church. He was not simply making ready for Christ's coming in history, the historical *parousia*—he is preparing the way of the Lord whenever the Lord comes to men. He went before Him even before birth; he went before Him in His public life; as Origen points out, he went before Him into the Kingdom of the Dead—and this is the most beautiful idea of all: that before Christ descended into Limbo to set the souls of the dead free John the Baptist had preceded Him there. And the Fathers of the Church tell us that he will come before Him on the Last Day, that he will announce the Lord at His last coming, to judge the living and the dead. He is the herald of every one of Christ's comings.

But we can also say that John the Baptist is always preparing the way of the Lord in the hearts of men and of nations. Since Christ is forever "He that is to come", since the whole history of the Church, from Ascension day to the Last Judgment, is the history of His *parousia* in the hidden world of men's souls, John is also forever going before Him, because the pattern of things in Christ's Incarnation is the pattern for everything that happens in His Mystical Body. Just as every grace comes to us through Mary, because she could not have borne Christ without being equally the mother of His Mystical Body, so in every conversion the way has been prepared by John the Baptist. That was the teaching of the Fathers. "I think," wrote Origen, "that the mystery (*sacramentum*) of John is still being carried out in the world. If a man is to believe in Jesus Christ, the spirit and power of John must first come into his soul and prepare for the Lord a perfect people, make the rough ways of the heart plain, make the crooked straight. Even now the spirit and power of John precede the coming of Our Lord and Saviour."[1]

Since the coming of Christ goes on forever—He is always He that is to come in the world and in the Church —there is always an Advent going on, and this Advent is filled by John the Baptist. It is John the Baptist's peculiar grace that he prepares the way for what is about to happen. It belongs to him specially to be there for the final preparation before every spiritual unfolding, every missionary development, every missionary awakening; and this grace of his is at work now. He it is who

[1] *Hom. Luc.*, iv; Rauer, p. 29, 1. 20–p. 30, 1. 8.

hastens the coming of Christ by sending out his resounding call to repentance, to conversion; and the power of his call makes men ready for Christ to come to them. It seems to me that we ought to feel this call of his as most specially pressing today, when for some countries at least this coming of Christ seems so urgent and so near.

II

THE MISSION OF THE ANGELS

ONE CHRISTIAN dogma which seems to have slid very much into the background nowadays is that of the angels. The Fathers in the first centuries were far more conscious than we are that human history fits into a far greater whole of spiritual history. The angels represent a tremendous broadening of our whole spiritual outlook, which is why I lay such stress on them. At a time when the limits of the visible world seem to be almost disappearing, when astronomers tell us of whole worlds of stars beyond the stars we see, of other, farther, milky ways, when they tell us that the starry universe expands indefinitely and spreads out forever in what we can only call space; at a time, too, when the history of the world seems to be going dizzily further and further back, and we are discovering that the world existed for millions and millions of years before man came on the scene at all; it really seems, in view of all this, that the picture Christianity gives is a very narrow one, because our interest turns merely on the history of mankind.

Now human history is obviously only the tiniest dot in the history of the material universe. But if we put it in its proper place, not within the visible cosmos, but in the spiritual cosmos, if we show that the Christian conception of things sees in fact an immense spiritual universe, made up of spiritual worlds of which mankind is just one, then our view of things takes on a grandeur, and a vastness which seems to me to answer one of the greatest needs of today. At a time when men are feeling conscious of the immensity of the universe, we can show that Christianity brings them into a universe mightier still. And I think that the theology of angels, by widening our view of the spiritual cosmos, is our means of doing this.

1. *The Liturgy of the Angels*

In Scripture we find different names given to different kinds of angels: Principalities, Thrones, Powers, Dominations (Eph. i. 21), Cherubim, Seraphim. The early Fathers put them all on the same level. The angels made up the fulness of the spiritual world. Origen and Gregory of Nyssa saw the whole of creation as numbering the hundred angels or angelic worlds: they were figured by the tabernacle Moses saw in vision on Sinai, which was an image of the world of heaven, that is to say of Christ in whose image all spiritual creation was made: "Everything in the description of the tabernacle—the columns, the rings, the cherubim, are the supernatural powers which are in the Word, and which keep the world going in accordance with the will of God."[1] Gregory of Nyssa tells how mankind once belonged to that angelic "pleroma", but fell from it. And Christ came to bring mankind back to the world of the angels, who stood by the gates of heaven waiting for their fallen sister to return.

So far there was no hierarchy. Clement of Alexandria was the first to see such an arrangement. He shows us all creation as a hierarchy, going from the Word to men, by way of the *Protoctistes*, archangels and angels. And he shows each order acting as intermediary between the orders above and below it.[2] Here again we find the

[1] Gregory of Nyssa, *Life of Moses.*
[2] *Eclogae propheticae*, P. G., ix, 1020 A.

influence of the Alexandrian schools of thought, and it was to be even more marked in Denys the Areopagite. It is to him that we owe what has become the classic division of the angels into nine choirs, made up of three groups of three orders each. And each order receives light from the one above, and passes it on to the order below: "The understandings of the first group, who are closest to God, led on by the splendours they receive as it were at first hand, are enlightened and perfected under the influence of a light at once ever more mysterious and ever clearer. The second hierarchy obeys the first, and commands the third; and the third is placed above the hierarchy of men. And thus in divine harmony and perfect proportion, each advances by help of the next towards Him who is the sovereign principle and end towards which everything is ordered."[1]

And Denys gives a most admirable description of the attributes of the different orders. Read what he says of the nature of the first hierarchy—Seraphim, Cherubim and Thrones:

They are most eminently pure, not merely in the sense that no blot, no stain, has ever marked them, and they are not constrained as we are by material imaginations, but chiefly because they cannot be touched by any principle of degradation. They are also contemplatives: I do not mean that they understand intellectual things by means of material symbols, but that they are bathed in a light far above mere intellectual knowledge. They are perfect, too, not because they can explain deep mysteries by using different symbols, but because their union with God is so lofty and so close that they get that high understanding of

[1] *The Hierarchy of Heaven*, x.

the things of God that it belongs to angels to have
(vii).

All the nostalgia the Greeks had for a world of intel-
ligibles is perfectly expressed in our theology of the angels.
What chiefly characterises eastern thought is that for it
the spiritual and eternal world is the most real. Plato's
idea of the world of ideas is an expression of this fact.
Now every civilisation will lay most stress on the aspect of
the Gospel that best fits in with its particular genius. To
the Greek genius it was necessary that there should be a
world of pure intelligences living outside time. Their
nostalgia for an intelligible world finds expression in the
knowledge of the world of angels. Plato saw true knowledge as contemplation of the Ideas. Greek mysticism saw
gnosis as both knowledge of God and contemplation of the
angelic world, with all its hierarchies and functions.
Mankind had once belonged to this celestial order. The
Christian gnostics thought that by contemplation they
would get back into that life with the angels, move with
them in the loftiest places, penetrate into- the inmost
secrets of things—at least during the brief moments when
by their contemplation they were lifted above the things
of earth.

This theology of a heavenly hierarchy was to be of
great help to all later theology. It delighted the Middle
Ages. We see this first of all from the great medieval
mystical writings—in Saint Bernard, Saint Thomas, Saint
Bonaventure. In his *De Consideratione* Saint Bernard goes
through all the categories of being and comes last to the
world of angels. He describes its hierarchies, whereupon
his soul is filled with longing, and he is carried away by
his wish to get to this homeland of his soul. Saint Thomas
devoted some very fine articles in the *Summa* to the angels.

He delves even further into their nature. The angels are not bound by the law of time, but have a sort of duration proper to their nature. They are not bound by space. They can act directly on the material world. But they cannot act directly upon other created intelligences. They do not know the future, nor the mysteries of grace, nor the secret thoughts of rational beings.[1]

It would be most interesting to trace the development of the theology of the angels through the history of art. Medieval art drew upon Denys's theology of the hierarchies: remember the doorway at Bourges, for example, where the angelic hierarchies surround Christ in glory, or Fra Angelico's "Coronation of Our Lady". But the art of the Counter-Reformation seems to give them still greater importance. There the most popular theme was the Ascension or the Assumption, showing all nature being lifted up towards the angelic world, as if it had lost its material weight. This helps to explain the tremendous mystical longing which characterised the period—as found, for instance, in Saint Teresa, Saint John of the Cross, Saint Francis of Sales. If you read the panegyrics on the saints written by Père Senault in the seventeenth century you will be struck by the extraordinary position given to the angels. And in this he is at one with the whole religious and cultural spirit of his time.

From what we read in Scripture it seems that the angels make up God's court. If it is God's glory to be known and loved by rational creatures, this is a sort of created radiance, and glory, which is always with Him. That is the impression we always get of the angels from the Old Testament. We see, for instance, at the beginning of the Book of Job, the sons of God coming before the Lord, and later filled with joy when He creates the world. In the

---

[1] For the theology of the angels, see Dom Vonier, *The Angels*.

same way in the Book of Daniel, when the prophet sees the Ancient of Days sitting on His throne, He is surrounded by a multitude of spirits: "Thousands of thousands ministered to him and ten thousand times a hundred thousand stood before him" (vii. 10). The Apocalypse, too, has much to say about angels when it describes the heavenly Jerusalem, which is their natural sphere: "And I beheld . . . many angels round about the throne, and the living creatures, and the ancients; and the number of them was thousands of thousands" (v. 11). Later on we see Christ coming forward as a conqueror, surrounded by the armies of heaven: "And he was clothed with a garment sprinkled with blood; and his name is called, THE WORD OF GOD. And the armies that are in heaven followed him on white horses, clothed in fine linen, white and clean" (xix. 13–14). Note how in all these texts the angelic world always appears as a multitude, so that to us it always has infinite perspectives.

The role of the angels, as they cluster about the Trinity, is primarily one of praise. They are the glory of God, and they give glory to God—that is to say, they bring back to Him the glory that is in them. This praise the angels give is the liturgy of heaven, which is the highest function of all spiritual creatures.[1] Saint John shows us this in the Apocalypse (vii. 11–12). Since Christ is the one universal high priest in heaven, and it is He who offers the one universal sacrifice, the angels are forever bound up in the offering. That is why they hold such a large place in our liturgy, particularly in the Mass.

The presence of the angels can be felt throughout the Mass. At the beginning, the Christian community on

[1] See Erik Peterson's excellent book, *Das Buch der Engeln*, on the subject of this liturgy of the angels.

earth humbles itself for its sins before all the saints in heaven, and before Michael the Archangel. The tremendous scene for the whole of Mass is thus set. In the *Gloria*, the hymn of the angels, we on earth associate ourselves with the liturgy of heaven. At High Mass it is through the intercession of Blessed Michael, standing at the right hand of the altar of incense, that we offer our incense as a symbol of all our prayers. The Preface links us up with all the hierarchies of heaven to sing the *Sanctus*, that most exalted of all angelic prayers in which the angels proclaim the utter holiness and infinity of God. And, at the solemn Epiclesis, after the Consecration, it is a mysterious Angel who bears our offering to the sublime altar of God.[1]

As I said, the *Sanctus* is the supreme prayer of the angels. And this is because their secondary function is to preserve, defend, keep all that is of God, all that touches God. They are the guardians of holiness, of consecration. And that is why they keep watch over everything that has been consecrated. In the first place, they stop anything impure from approaching God. Thus it was that after the first sin a cherub was stationed at the gateway of Paradise, which was the realm of grace, to prevent anyone going in, with that sword of fire which was at once the fire of purgatory and of holiness, which allowed no stain, left no sin unconsumed.

Whenever God has manifested Himself to mankind He has always come with angels in attendance to see that nothing defiled should touch Him. That is the function of those cherubim described by Ezechiel, and in the psalms God is described as "he that sitteth upon the cherubim", to show how far above all created things He is (Ps. lxxix.

[1] Origen stressed this presence of the angels in Christian worship. See Daniélou, *Origen*.

2; xcviii. i). It is they who prevent anything profane
from coming near Him. Thus, on Isaias' vision—to
which any discussion of holiness must bring us back—
Saint Bernard comments: "With two of these wings they
veil His head: these are the raptures of wonder into which
they are plunged by contemplating God, and of veneration
which gives them a share in His glory. These wings screen
God so that the wicked cannot look upon Him. They are
dazzled by the wings, but instead of this raising their
minds, it only rouses envy in them".[1]

Just as the angels surround God, as a sort of screen for
His holiness, in the same way they watch over everything
that is consecrated to Him; round it, too, they set up that
rampart of fire, that mysterious *aura*, that temple. They
dwell in the Church, the House of God, creating the
atmosphere of worship. (Remember how Heliodorus was
scourged by angels for his sacrilege, in 2 Maccabees iii.
22–30). That was what Saint Paul meant in that curious
phrase that women must have their heads covered in
Church "because of the angels" (1 Cor. xi. 10). They
are the guardian angels, guarding the temples of our
souls. It is they who throw a sort of protective radiance
about the innocence of children: "See that you despise
not one of these little ones, for I say to you that their
angels in heaven always see the face of my Father who is in
heaven" (Matt. xviii. 10).

2. *The Angels and the Nations*

Ruysbroeck describes God to us as "a perpetual movement of flux and reflux, the Unity forever going outwards
into Trinity, and the Trinity forever drawing together

[1] *De Verb. Isaiae III ad finem.*

into Unity".[1] This law of divine life is the same law that governs the whole spiritual creation. The lives of the great saints are all made up of the perpetual flux and reflux that Saint Bernard describes, in which the call of souls is always drawing the apostle away from his contemplation of God, and contemplation is always drawing him back from the apostolate into divine union. The same law holds good in the angelic world. They are the *Liturgi* or attendants, of whom the Fathers speak, whose work is to adore the Blessed Trinity. But they are also the *Angeli*, the messengers, who dispense God's gifts and announce His designs. And they are more blest than we, in that they can fulfil their missions without ever having to stop contemplating the face of God. In this they set before the apostle the ideal he must always be tending towards of a perfect union of action and contemplation, or, better still, action so totally bound up in God's will that it becomes at the same time contemplation of the mystery of the Redemption. We shall see this later on, when we look at prophetic contemplation.

According to Christian tradition the role of the angels as instruments of the works of God starts with the actual mechanism of the visible world. In the Apocalypse Saint John shows them in charge of the elements—fire (xiv. 18), and water (xvi. 5). This is merely an echo of a far older Jewish tradition. In the Book of Enoch there are angels in charge of the sun, moon and stars (xliii. 2). They order the movement of lightning and thunder, they keep the sea within its bounds (lx. 2). They watch over waters and winds, the dew and the rain (lx. 21). Judaism attributed so much to the angels, in fact, that Saint Paul had to warn against excesses (Gal. iv. 9; Col. ii. 18). All the Old Testament tells us was to be developed further in Christian

[1] *Royaume des amis de Dieu.*

tradition. Athenagoras wrote that "God, the Creator and Demiurge of the world, through the intermediary of His Word, divided up and placed the angels to look after the elements, the heavens, the world and everything in it, and see that all worked in harmony".[1] Origen takes up the same notion: "There are angels in charge of everything, of earth as well as air and fire, that is to say, all the elements. They are also the instruments the Word uses in governing all the animals and plants, and the stars of the sky".[2] Thus "if it were not for the presence of invisible administrators the earth would not bear what we say it produces by nature, water would not spring up and run in fountains and streams, the air would not remain pure and give life to all who breathe it".[3]

But the work in which the angels are most particularly associated by the Word is the highest work of all—the work of Revelation and Redemption. Their part in it began in the Old Testament. The angels came and went between God and mankind, they were the instruments of His graces. In Genesis we see them accompanying God when He appeared to Abraham in human form in the vale of Mambre (Gen. xviii. 1 ff). That lovely passage about Jacob's ladder shows them going up and down between heaven and earth (xxviii. 10–22). From the New Testament we learn that it was through them that the law was given to Moses: "The law . . . was ordained by angels in the hand of a mediator" (Gal. iii. 19. See Acts vii. 53). The same thing had been taught earlier by Judaism (Jubilees i. 27–9).[4] The role accorded to the angels in the Old Testament shows how far inferior it is to

[1] *Apol.*, x.
[2] *Hom. Jos.*, x, 6.
[3] *Contra Celsum*, viii, 31.
[4] See also Deuteronomy xxxiii. 2.

the New. It is Christ Himself who "being made better than the angels" (Heb. i. 4), was to promulgate the New Law. The angels, then, play the part of "missionaries"—they are those who prepare the ways of the Lord: "Behold I send my angel, and he shall prepare the way before my face" (Mal. iii. 1). They are brought in at the very beginning, the foreshadowing of the works of salvation. By their inspirations, they prepare men's souls to receive the Word who follows them.

But was their mysterious work of preparation concerned only with Israel? Christian tradition thinks otherwise. It considers that angels are given charge over all the nations to prepare them to receive God's Revelation. And here we can be strictly accurate when we speak of a missionary theology of the angels. This doctrine has its starting point in the theology of the Septuagint. Thus we read in Deuteronomy: "When the Most High divided to the nations their inheritance . . . he set the bounds of the people according to the number of the children of Israel" (xxxii. 8), which reads, in the Septuagint translation, "the number of the angels of God"; this translation is a true interpretation of the text, and underlies a whole tradition of thought on the subject. Various Hebrew writers developed it. The *Testament of Nephtali* tells how, before the dispersal of the nations, Michael asked each one to choose an angel. The seventy shepherds in the *Book of Enoch* were the angels set over the pagan nations. This same tradition was taken up by the Fathers of the Church. Origen writes that "the Lord's share is Jacob, and His lot is Israel, and the other nations fall to the lot of the angels", commenting on the text of Deuteronomy.[1] And elsewhere he says: "We are not allowed to believe that wicked angels preside over the nations and that those same nations are

[1] *De princ.*, i, 5, 2.

not also entrusted to good angels".[1] And he shows us what was the position of the angels before the coming of Christ: "Certain shepherds must be considered as angels to whom men are entrusted. And each angel took trouble to watch over those in his charge, but needed help if they were to be well governed".[2]

These excerpts bring us to the very heart of the drama of paganism and the meaning of missionary work. Pagan nations are in some mysterious sense protected by angels who have been placed over them by God to guard them, punish them, dispose them towards what is good. It is thinkable that the "demon" Socrates spoke of was the angel of Greece, that Buddha, Zoroaster, Gandhi, Tagore and the rest were not unaided by angels in reaching the heights they did. But at the same time the pagan nations all have their demons, who get themselves adored under the form of idols or false gods, and hold them in bondage.[3] And it is they who are responsible for the errors which even among the best pagans get mixed in with the truth that comes to them from the angels.[4] Before Christ came on earth the angels of the nations were quite powerless to set the nations in their charge free of their demons. They longed earnestly, then, for Christ's coming, praying in the name of the pagan peoples, foreshadowing the perfect praise in the world to come, hastening the coming of the Liberator by their desires and petitions. In this they are the perfect models and patterns for apostolic souls, to whose care Christ today entrusts the nations He has now bought with His blood, so that until these, too, shall be brought into the unity of the Church they may bring

---

[1] *Hom. Luc.*, xiii.

[2] *Hom. Luc.*, xiii. I have gone into this more thoroughly in *Origen*, p. 222 ff.

[3] Origen, *Hom. Gen.*, ix, 3; *Contra Celsum*, v, 30.

[4] Origen, *De Princ.*, iii, 3, 2–3.

them closer to Christ, interceding for them, and hastening the day of their redemption.

In the Old Testament, and with pagan peoples, the presence of angels is a sign of estrangement from God. In the New Testament, as Gerhard Kittel so profoundly notes, they are a sign that He is present.[1] For they are the intelligible radiance of the Word, the manifestation of His glory. And just as they surround Him in His eternal pre-existence, so they go with Him in His mission in the world, becoming missionaries with Him.

The Gospels, too, are full of them. And if we notice them little, it is chiefly because, just as Christ veils the glory of His divinity in the Incarnation, so the angels keep in the background of the drama being enacted. But the heavenly host are always present, always ready to be called upon: "Thinkest thou that I cannot ask my Father and he will give me presently more than twelve legions of angels?" (Matt. xxvi. 53). It is of the nature of the angels to efface themselves before the Lord of angels and never draw attention to themselves. Here again they are a model to missionaries, whose great struggle must always be against drawing souls to themselves; they must always be leading them to Christ and themselves fading into the background. That was how John the Baptist behaved: "He must increase, I must decrease." Now Christ speaks of John the Baptist as the angel who went before His face. That is how the missionary should act. The work he is doing is not his own: it is not even his country's. The wicked angels of the nations will always find a way to make the Gentiles adore them, and one way is in the cult of the nation, of which they are a sort of personification. The true missionary will, if necessary, become one with those

[1] *Theol. Wort.*, Art. *Angelos.*

he is working among, that he may conquer them all to Christ.

The contemplative always sees beyond the visible world; to him the mysteries of Christ appear in their reality as heavenly events surrounded with all the glory of the angels, as something far beyond their mere sensible effects. In Altdorffer's "Nativity", for instance, you see the humble Virgin giving suck to her child, but, beyond, the skies go back and back to show the worlds of angels adoring. Gabriel is the angel of annunciations. It was he who revealed the mysteries of Christ's coming to Daniel. It was he who appeared to Zachary in the Temple, and who came to the Virgin of Nazareth just before the Word Himself. Angels were present at the Nativity to tell the good news to the shepherds and sing the *Gloria in Excelsis*. At every crucial point in the Gospel they are there. They come to minister to Jesus after His temptations, which gives us a sort of echo of the spiritual struggle that took place around the Word in heaven, long before the history of earth had begun to be, between Michael's forces and the angels of Satan. They strengthen Jesus at the time of His agony, when He is undergoing His final combat with the Prince of this world: "And there appeared to him an angel from heaven, strengthening him" (Luke xxii. 43). They proclaim the glory of the risen Christ to Magdalen and the other holy women. They were with Christ when He ascended, and was raised above all the worlds of angels to the right hand of His Father (Eph. i. 20–1). And at the end of time they will come with Him, this time as a dazzling manifestation of the glory of the Word at His last great coming on earth.

But between the Ascension and the last coming of Christ comes a long space of time, filled by the Church. This time is, above all, a time of mission. It is the time when the salvation of mankind, which has been in substance won by Christ, must be made available to all nations. Here again the angels of the nations have a part to play. They received Christ at His coming with joy. They had toiled long and with poor results for the pagan nations. Origen saw the shepherds in the Gospel as figures of the shepherds of the nations, to whom the angels of the Nativity announced the birth of Christ: "Certain shepherds must be considered to be the angels to whom men's souls are entrusted. They all needed help if the nations in their charge were to be governed well. Therefore the angel came to tell them that Jesus was born, that the true Shepherd had come. There was, for instance, a Shepherd of Macedonia. He needed help from God. That was why a Macedonian appeared to Paul. The shepherds had need of Christ's coming. His coming into the world was a tremendous joy to those who had nations under their care. . . . The angel who directed the affairs of Egypt made great capital out of Christ's descent from heaven in converting the Egyptians. For before Christ came the angels could do little to help those in their care".[1] On the other hand, the wicked princes of the nations, their power taken from them by Christ's cross (Col. ii. 15) try to fight against His Kingdom.[2]

Henceforth the angels of the nations are working with the Apostles to put Christ's victory into effect for their peoples: "The Apostles have angels to help them carry out their work of preaching, and to achieve the spreading of the good news."[3] "Peter has an angel, and so does Paul, and so do all the Apostles and lesser ministers".[4] If, on

---

[1] *Hom. Luc.*, xiii.
[2] "You also were part of some prince's share. Jesus came and snatched you away from the evil power. But each of us has an adversary who is trying to draw us away to his own prince" (*Hom. Luc.*, xxxv).
[3] *Hom. Num.*, xi, 4.   [4] *ibid.*

the one hand, the Apostles are always coming up against the princes of the nations, and if their mission seems simply a spiritual struggle to free men from the powers that hold them in thrall, they also know that they can count on the help of the angels, who are their allies as it were behind the enemy's lines, secretly preparing souls to receive the word they are coming to give. Saint Paul shows us the angel of the Macedonians appearing, and asking him to come and evangelise Europe. In the same way angels called upon Juste de Bretennières to set off to convert Japan. Thus the angels of the pagan nations are always making their sad call heard—in the silence of souls in contemplation, in the hearts of pure children, in everyone capable of hearing them—as they ask for apostles to come and help them set the captive nations free.

3. *Discernment of Spirits*

They are bound up with the apostles in the work of converting souls; they also work with them in forming and building up the Church. There are then, also, angels of the Churches. "Just as in a city where there are as yet no born Christians, if someone arrives, and begins to instruct, train and bring to the faith the men of that city, he becomes the bishop of those whom he has taught, so, too, the angels will later be the princes of those they have brought in from the various nations, and raised to God by their work and ministrations".[1] In this way each Church has a visible Bishop and an invisible Angel, who rival each other in zeal.[2] Note how in this passage the bishopric is clearly seen as a carrying on of the apostolate. And just

---

[1] *Hom. Num.*, xi, 4.
[2] *Hom. Luc.*, xiii.

as they take charge of the Churches, so of all baptised souls: "Come forward, O angel, receive him who has been converted from the ancient error, from the teachings of evil spirits; like a physician, nurse and instruct him; he is a tiny child; take him, and give him the baptism of second birth".[1] So there are guardian angels who help the souls in their charge in all sorts of ways, laying their prayers before God, and conveying His inspirations to them. But note here, too, that the angels are always working against the action of demons. In fact, just as every man has an angel guardian, he also has a demon guardian: "Every man has two angels, the good one who leads him to what is right, the wicked one leading him to evil."[2] Before baptism, the good angel was almost powerless and the evil spirit held sway over the soul; after baptism it is just the opposite, but the conquered demon still tries to delay the soul on its path to holiness.[3]

The whole doctrine of the action of spirits is involved here, and it is a most important part of traditional Christian spirituality. Saint Ignatius Loyola states it very well in his rules for the discernment of spirits, which are a psychological counterpart of the dogmatic meditation on the two standards. For the soul in sin, the good spirit's work is to suggest remorse, whereas the evil spirit tries to reassure him. But when a soul is going towards God it is just the opposite. "The evil spirit saddens, paralyses, upsets him, whereas the good spirit gives him courage and strength, consolation, tears, inspirations and peace, making it easier for him, removing all the obstacles." The

[1] *Hom. Ezech.*, i, 7. Concerning Origen's teaching on the action of the angels in our spiritual life see Dom Bettencourt *Doctrina Ascetica Origenis*, Rome, 1947, which treats the subject fully.

[2] *Hom. Luc.*, xiii.

[3] Bettencourt [*ibid.*] speaks as if the good angel simply took the place of the evil, which is not so.

interesting thing is that this doctrine can be found from the earliest days of the Church. Origen goes into it at some length: "We know that the thoughts of our heart come, sometimes from ourselves, sometimes from the inspiration of adverse powers, sometimes from God or His angels."[1]

Too often we read Athanasius' *Life of Saint Antony* only for its historical value, but actually what it is chiefly concerned to teach is this same doctrine of the discernment of spirits.[2] It is possible and easy to distinguish between the presence of good and bad angels if God gives one the grace. There is nothing disturbing about seeing good angels. The effect is calm and soothing, so that joy, alacrity and courage are infused into the soul. One's thoughts remain untroubled, undisturbed. The soul is seized with a desire for the things of heaven. Whereas the inroads and appearances of evil spirits are troubling. They are accompanied by noise, uproar, cries, rather like an uprising of a mob, or of brigands, which produce terror of soul, disturbance and disorders in the thoughts, fear of death, and finally evil desires.[3] Saint Gregory of Nyssa, another of Origen's disciples, echoes this teaching: Those who practise virtue can take advantage of the help their nature offers to God, a help which existed before, which began, in fact, when they were born, but which they do not realise is there until they become more familiar with the supernatural life. Man finds himself placed between two companions who have totally opposed intentions. The good spirit works in the soul by showing the reward to be hoped for, by communicating a taste for God's gifts, whereas the other only offers pleasures of sense from which

[1] *De Princ.*, iii, 2, 4.
[2] See Louis Bouyer, *La Vie de Saint Antoine et la spiritualité du monachisme primitive* (an unpublished thesis).
[3] *Life of Saint Antony*, 37.

nothing good can be got, and which serve only to bind weak souls more firmly to earth.[1]

This action of the angels is always most in evidence when a soul is beginning in the spiritual life. Their role is always one of preparation. They do as it were the spade work. They make the soul ready. In this way they prepared the soul of Mary to receive the Word. In this way they prepared all mankind, educating them under the Old Testament, to receive the Word; as Origen says, they "cared for the Bride who was as yet only a child"; in this way they prepare the ways of the Lord among peoples who are still pagan. Exactly the same thing happens in the spiritual life. "It may be," wrote Origen, "that frightened children need angels; and that, to those who are more advanced, it is the Lord of the angels Himself who says, 'I am with him in tribulation.' As long as we are imperfect, and still need help to free us from our sins, what we need is an angel; but once grown up, when we have passed the stage of being under teachers and tutors, we can be led forward by Christ Himself."[2] Thus the history of each soul exactly reproduces the history of all mankind; there, too, the angels were the tutors of the child, humanity, until in Mary it was ready to receive the Word Himself. Gregory of Nyssa tells us the same thing: "When one has passed a certain stage it is clear that the fraternal help of an angel is no longer enough in the struggles that now present themselves." Saint Ignatius, too, makes a distinction between the consolations we get from angels, and the higher ones which can only come from God: "Only God can give us consolation without making use of the means one would ordinarily expect."

And this brings us back once more to just what is the nature of the angels. They are present everywhere, every-

[1] *Life of Moses*, n. 67. [2] *Com. Matt.*, xiii, 26.

where hidden. That is how they appear in Scripture. That is how they are in the world. That is how they are present to our souls. They do not want to keep any homage or honour for themselves, but simply to spread the glory of God by leading His spiritual creatures to Him. In the course of its journey, the soul comes upon the angelic world, into which contemplation brings it back. But its contemplation never stops there. They are the watchmen of the city whom the Sulamite meets on her way, and of whom she asks for her Beloved, and who, according to Gregory of Nyssa, show by their silence that He whom she seeks is above all power of naming. Here, too, then, they are the perfect models of the Apostles, carrying out their ministry without ever ceasing to contemplate the Trinity, never stained by their contact with the world, wanting only to bring souls to Christ, and then merge into the background, keeping nothing for themselves.

III

THE PART played by Our Lady in the whole economy of salvation and in the inner life of every Christian, is coming more and more into view in contemporary Catholic life. Some people are worried by this, because it seems to widen the gulf between us and our Protestant brethren. But if, as I think, we are, in our Mariology, faithful to the inspiration of the Holy Ghost, tending gradually over the course of years to a more exact understanding of the truth contained in Holy Scripture, then this cannot prove a lasting cause of separation between Christians. What I should like to show in the pages that follow is that the function the Catholic Church gives to Mary, in all essentials—and I shall not go into all the various forms of devotion that have grown up around it—is not something we are adding to the teaching of Scripture, nor a throwback to paganism, nor the sublimation of this or that instinct, but something that comes to us from the mind of the Word of God Himself, as it comes to be more clearly understood over the course of centuries by the faith of the community and the tradition of the Magisterium, acted upon by the Holy Ghost, who is always at work in the Church. What we are dealing with is one of the most mysterious of all truths—no concession to reason, but rather a grave difficulty for reason—that a woman was chosen to be the Mother of God, and that, according to God's unchangeable plan, this woman was to have the same relationship to the members of Christ as she had to Christ Himself. And if, as I intend to try here, we can show people that Our Lady's role tied in with all that had gone before in the Old Testament, that will be the best way to justify our view of the part she still plays in history, and especially in preparing the nations which are still in expectation of the coming of Christ.

1. *Mary and the Old Testament*

The Blessed Virgin had a most crucial role in the first coming of Christ. In her culminated all the expectation of the Jewish people, insofar as all the preparations, aspirations, inspirations, graces, prefigurations which had filled the Old Testament, all came together and were summed up in her; it is true to say that at the eve of Christ's coming she was the epitome and incarnation of the long waiting of twenty centuries. The whole of the Old Testament seems to come together in her with a more ardent longing and a more complete spiritual preparation for Our Lord's coming. *Omnis vallis implebitur, et omnis collis humiliabitur.* "Every valley shall be filled, and every mountain and hill shall be brought low." The work of the Old Testament was one of education: mankind, rugged, coarse, as yet unformed, still utterly carnal-minded, must be made able, bit by bit, to take God's gifts, to receive the Holy Ghost. It was a long, progressive work of training. And the training culminated in the soul of the Blessed Virgin; and if we can say that in some sense her soul is outside time, and that in her eternity is present, then we may also say that she was prepared by the education of the whole of her people: she is the marvellous flower sprung out of Israel, the final point in the mysterious work of the Holy Ghost in the souls of all the prophets and all the holy women of Israel. All that was done in the soul of Sara, in the soul of Rebecca, in the soul of Rachel, in the soul of Ruth, all that was accomplished in the souls of all the great women of the Old Testament, was brought to its perfect fulness in the soul of Mary. It is, in fact, absolutely true to say that in her "every valley was filled, every mountain and hill brought low". That is to say, in her Our Lord's path was smooth before Him.

What was this education that Israel, and through Israel all mankind, had to be given that it might become a fit path for Our Lord? They must first be given a sense of God. Primitive Israel had no sense of God, or, rather, had a totally wrong and gross conception of Him. To them everything was God, and yet nothing was God. Primitive mankind tended to divinise everything, but never came near the true God. To them the smallest stone that stood up, the smallest tree on a hilltop, the smallest spring, was a hidden and wonderful presence of something divine. It was, fundamentally, idolatrous, adoring the creature as if it were creator.

The first step in the Holy Spirit's education of humanity was, then, to wean it from idol-worship, and lead it to acknowledge and recognise the one true God. Throughout the history of the Jews we feel the tension going on, the people forever hankering after their idols. Whenever they came in contact with the Egyptians, the Chanaanites, the Babylonians, we see how they are drawn, how the primitive element comes forward, because they were still carnal, still close to carnal nature. God used a sort of violence to drag them away from their naturist leanings, from the powers of earth and of plants, to lead them back to recognising the one Holy God, who is a transcendant, a devouring God, a God who is, in a way, hard to bear for a humanity as yet fragile, new, for whom the weight of God is almost too heavy. That was what Rilke meant when he said of the angels: "Their presence is the first degree of the terrible."[1] Mankind must try to get used to bearing God, although His weight on their shoulders is so great that they try at first to get away from it. Throughout the history of Israel God is constantly reproaching His people for being unfaithful, because they went to adore in high places and under every green tree. In chapter xvi of the book of Ezechiel they are told: "And ... after all thy wickedness ... thou didst also build thee a common stew and madest thee a brothel house in every street. At every head of the way thou hast set up a sign of thy prostitution, and hast made thy beauty to be abominable, and hast prostituted thyself to every one that passed by, and hast multiplied thy fornications." Israel had been given the honour of being chosen the only bride of Iahweh, and every turning to false gods was unfaithfulness to Him.

It was quite the contrary with the Blessed Virgin; she came at the end of this long, slow process of education, and had the perfect sense of God and His unity. If we compare her fidelity with Israel's infidelity, we see how the mystery of the education of Israel was being perfectly fulfilled in her: she is the *Virgo fidelis*, the faithful virgin, who was never anything but faithful, whose fidelity was the perfect answer to the fidelity of God; she was always entirely consecrated to the one true God. The liturgy, then, is quite right to apply to her the words of the spouse in the Canticle, for it is the epithalamion for the marriage of the Word with His people, the poem of the Covenant, and she it was who, after so many infidelities, gave, by her fidelity, all mankind's answer to the faithfulness of God. One might say that this aspect of Our Lady is the one most closely connected with the Father, the source of the unity in the Trinity.

[1] *Duino Elegies*, i, 3.

This mystery of the education of Israel is, in the second place, the mystery of grace, the giving of divine life to mankind. And we can see that, at the beginning, Israel had no notion that this was what was happening. They thought God had chosen them to give them temporal goods, to lead them out of the slavery of Egypt where their life was so hard, where they made bricks out of mud and ground up straw under Egyptian overseers; they thought that God led them across the desert simply to give them the promised land, a land literally flowing with milk and honey, milk for them to drink, honey to eat— a land of plump cows, giving birth to fine calves, a land of bees whose honey would feed the children of Israel. This was what they were interested in, this what they hoped for from God. And God, in His goodness and patience, God, who knows His creatures—"for I know what man is"—and takes men for what they are, took mankind as it was at the beginning, just as He takes each of us as we are at our beginnings, and to draw them to Him, gave them at first what they wanted. Therefore, once He had chosen His people, He promised them first a certain happiness on earth; then, having given them various goods, He tried bit by bit to make them understand that these were not the things that mattered, and gradually began to withdraw these things from them; little by little He was putting the mystery of the Cross into the mystery of Israel—that mystery by which He takes from us the things we are too fond of, so that by emptying us of self He can fill us with Himself.

You find this mystery at the very core of Jewish history: it is the mystery of the just man suffering, which we find in the Book of Job, that strange book in the very heart of the Old Testament, the mystery of a soul being tried by God when it does not itself see what evil it has done—

a thing both repugnant and meaningless to the Jewish mind. Job himself did not as yet know what the answer was. He could only cling to his knowledge of his own innocence, and adore God's plan which he did not understand. The plan was in fact quite intelligible and extremely wise: God was teaching Job, and through him all his people, that He had never promised His friends the goods of this world; remember what Pius XI said at the canonisation of a certain Italian saint: that to see what God thinks of the goods of this world you have only to look at the people He gives them to; He can hardly have bound Himself to give them to His friends since He gives them so liberally to His enemies as well. The inequality with which the goods of this world are distributed, which has no relation at all to the order of merit, is proof positive that God attaches no importance to them, and that the real goods are goods of the spirit. Throughout the history of Israel God was trying to detach His people from material goods, and lead them to see that it was goods of quite a different kind that He had in store for them. But we know how hard the people found it to understand this teaching, for when Christ at last came the Jews were disappointed; they hoped for an earthly king who would give them power over other nations, but instead of such glory they saw a crucifix. And even on the eve of the Ascension the Apostles asked Christ: "Lord, wilt thou at this time restore again the kingdom to Israel?"

In Our Lady we see the perfectly successful result of this education. Saint Bernard says of her that the only thing she ever asked for was grace: *Et semper inveniet gratiam.* She did not imitate Solomon by asking for wisdom. She asked for grace because grace is the one thing we need. She was, therefore, perfectly wise; in her, that is to say, the work of wisdom was perfectly accomplished; and, being perfectly wise,—and *sapientia* means the same as *recta sapere*, to savour the right things, to savour the things of the spirit—because she had the taste for spiritual things, she asked for grace and got it. *Ave Maria, gratia plena*. She was blessed to hear those wonderful words: "(Thou art) full of grace." Why "full of grace"? Because she wanted grace, and wanted only grace, because she fully understood that "but one thing is necessary", and therefore obtained it. Here again she was the perfect fulfilment of God's education of Israel.

And, finally, God wanted to teach the Jews that He was the God of all men, and not simply of Israel. That is perhaps the high point of the whole drama, that is where the "stiff-necked race" found it hardest to accept God's plan for it; it is certainly the great paradox of that plan. God began by choosing Israel; for nineteen centuries Israel was the only one, and despised all other peoples, who had, indeed, not been so chosen; yet still, bit by bit, God tried to make this people He had chosen understand that He had not chosen them for themselves, but to be an instrument for carrying out His designs in regard to the other nations. At first Israel took this to mean that they were to exercise dominion over the others, that they were always to be in the first place. Only gradually did they see God's plan—that they were to prepare for the Saviour's coming, but that once He had come they were to fade into the background among all the other nations of the earth. And this was what they could not accept; they refused to join the ranks as one nation among all the others.

In Our Lady we see quite the reverse; in her, the fruit of the Jewish people, we see acceptance of the plan, and universal charity. She was not only a daughter of Israel, but she was the one through whom Israel flowed back into the common human current; she was at once daughter of David and of Abraham, and *Mater divinae gratiae*, universal mediatrix, mother of all mankind. She fully realised the promise made to Israel that they would have a special work to do which should affect the whole race. And Mary, born of the race of Abraham, forever a Jewess, is at the same time the mother of all men. She was the one who accepted to be no longer only a Jew, who allowed her heart to expand to the bounds of the earth, who renounced the privilege of her birth, only to receive a far greater privilege of universality. The Blessed Virgin, the culmination of Jewish history, is the perfect thing that God intended that history to produce.

This gives us the key to the suffering of her heart. What died in Mary's heart on the eve of Christ's Passion was the merely human love she still had for Christ as her human son: what was born in her heart on the day He rose was her universal motherhood of all men. For this to happen, it is quite true to say that something in her heart had to die: it was the end of a great happiness, of the thirty-three years she had lived with God made man. That is why, when Christ indicating John, said to her, "Woman, behold thy son", a sword pierced deep into her heart, it was the end of a marvellous reality; at that moment she went beyond the love concentrated on the humanity of Jesus, she opened her heart wide enough to include the whole of humanity; this could only be done by death, by that death of the heart, by as deep a suffering in her heart as Our Lord had in His Body; for this, too, this growth of charity, this outgoing of love that was to embrace the world, could only come about through death. In each of our lives it comes about through death, when we go beyond our own narrow limits to enlarge our hearts to the compass of Christ's heart; and just the same thing happens in the history of every nation inasmuch as, to enter into the body of Christ, it too must go beyond its own particular narrowness, give up its imperialism. This is just one aspect of the mystery of Christ drawing all things together by His cross.

2. *Mary and the Church*

All this, which was simply the preparation and fore-shadowing of Christ in Our Lady's soul, is a reality still present to us, for the mystery we are now living in the world is the mystery of Christ's gradual coming into all souls, into all nations. Christ had appeared in the flesh, the culmination of Israel's hopes; Mary had seen Him for whom she had waited, she had held in her arms the child born in Bethlehem, and with Simeon had been able to salute Him as a Light to enlighten the Gentiles. Christ, then, had certainly come. He has come, but He is always He that is to come. He has come, but not yet wholly come; and though the waiting of Israel had been crowned, Israel is nonetheless still waiting. We live always during Advent, we are always waiting for the Messias to come. He has come, but is not yet fully manifest. He is not fully manifest in each of our souls; He is not fully manifest in mankind as a whole: that is to say, that just as Christ was born according to the flesh in Bethlehem of Juda so must He be born according to the spirit in each of our souls. The whole mystery of the spiritual life is that Jesus is forever being born in us. We have got to be always transforming ourselves into Christ, taking on the disposi-tions of His heart, the judgments of His mind; for the whole meaning of being a Christian is to become bit by bit transformed into Jesus Christ, so that we truly become children of His Father, for the only real children of the Father are those who have fully "put on" the Son, and the mystery of the Christian life is that each soul becomes Christ. In the same way Christ has not fully come in regard to mankind as a whole; though He has come in certain peoples, He has not come in others. There are whole stretches of humanity in which Christ has never been born. The mystical Christ is not yet complete. He is still incomplete, lacking members, and the perfect missionary prayer is for Christ to come in the whole world, for His body to attain its fulness of stature.

Now what is true of the preparation for Christ's coming in the flesh is also true of the spiritual preparation for His coming in our souls, and the preparation for His spiritual coming in the whole Mystical Body, for God's plan is a unity. And just as Mary played a leading part—and this leading part is the essence of her being—and a part shared by no one else in regard to Christ's physical birth, since the flesh He took He took of her, so Mary goes on playing a leading part in preparing for every subsequent coming of Christ. We can say with the Fathers that Mary still moves about the world, so as to be there always to prepare for the coming of Christ. She does this, first of all, in each of our souls. It is absolutely true to say that Mary has a special part in our spiritual lives, because she it is who prepares for Christ's coming in us, and who, bit by bit, forms Christ in our souls. This work of Mary's fits in with the spirit of spiritual childhood. But just as the spirit of childhood is in no way a sublimation of the nostalgia for childhood, so devotion to Mary is in no way a sublimation of human motherhood. Mary's part in God's design is far from being a humanisation of Christianity; it is in fact one of the aspects of the Incarnation which human reason finds it hardest to take to, and that is why all forms of rationalism try to do away with it. To accept it is to become one of those spiritual children to whom God gave the promises of His Kingdom.

But besides this relationship to individuals, she also has a part to play in the coming of Christ to peoples He has not yet come to. This is most especially the missionary aspect of the mystery of Mary. The mystery of Our Lady is that she was there before Jesus was; she was in Israel before Him. And in her Jesus was in some mysterious way present to Israel before He came, for she was totally in union with Him, there was nothing in her that was not for Him. She was there, then, in that time before the Incarnation. And it seems as if in some way the Church must have been there, for Mary was a figure of the Church, of mankind redeemed by Christ, before ever Jesus was born. And mysteriously, too, in the time between the Ascension and Pentecost, when Jesus was not there, having gone to His glory, He was still somehow there, because she was. And although the Church as such did not begin to exist until after Pentecost, yet the Church was in some way there, too. Not until Pentecost did the Holy Ghost come to dwell in the Apostles and form them into a hierarchical Church; but the Church was there before that, for Mary was there.

We can see, then, the part Our Lady is to play among pagan peoples: the Church has not come to them, Jesus has not yet come to them, yet the Church is there, because Mary is. Until, then, these pagan peoples are converted to Christ, until the visible Church has taken root among them, Mary will be mysteriously present, preparing, pre-figuring the Church, anticipating all that the Church will be. That is the deep and mysterious bond between Mary and the pagan nations. Do you remember Péguy's

explaining that though he cannot say "Our Father" he
can still say "Hail Mary"? A great many sinners cannot
say the "Our Father" who can still say the *Ave Maria*.
There is some justice in it; you may not be worthy to say
the "Our Father" if you are not in the proper filial dispositions, if you are not in a state of grace, and yet it
seems that even then you can still say the "Hail Mary",
for though Jesus and His grace have not returned to you,
Our Lady is still there. That is why Mary has a special
relationship with sinners; and it is this relationship which
is making itself felt when a sinner says he can pray to
Mary but cannot yet approach Christ.

In the same way Mary is present to the nations which
are still in darkness; Christ and His Church have not yet
come, but Mary is with them. That is why the nations
that do not yet know Christ have Our Lady's special
protection and preparation. We can pray to her specially
for them. We know she is a channel of grace. Theology
teaches that as well as sanctifying grace there is something
called prevenient grace; that is to say, that before we are
in a state of grace we need not be totally without any kind
of grace, that there are graces for those who have not yet
got sanctifying grace, graces which prepare them for
Grace; indeed, if there were no such graces we should
never receive sanctifying grace at all, for there is no other
way to it. Now this we can compare to Mary's work.
She is the grace where Grace has not yet come, the prevenient grace, the grace which prepares. That is why we
can speak of her peculiar relationship with pagan peoples.
They now are in the position the Jews were in before
Christ came, where the Apostles were before they had
received the Holy Ghost, before the Church was visibly
constituted.

Here and there we catch a glimpse of Mary's presence.

Indeed, in Islam it is more than a hidden presence. Though the Mussulmans do not give Christ all the recognition due to Him, they do give great homage to Mary. Surely, then, she must one day bring them to Him. They are the only descendants of Abraham who recognise and proclaim her purity. What a glimpse we get here of history rooted in God, and here in Mary, too. Abraham had two sons, to whom the Holy Land was promised: and the descendants of Isaac, of whom Mary is the glory— *Tu gloria Jerusalem, tu laetitia Israel*—have blasphemed her of whom the Holy Land is but a figure, treating her as an adulteress, a loose woman, whereas the race of Ismael declare her virginity. It was the race of Ismael who held the promised land for the last thirteen hundred years, while a fiery sword kept the race of Isaac out of the lost Paradise of the Promise. And today more than ever that land is a sign of contradiction between the two sons of Abraham; yet one day they will both be united in recognising her of whom the material reality of that land was always only a figure, they will have learnt how true it is that "the letter killeth, but the spirit quickeneth".

In the Far Eastern civilisations, too, we find Mary present—more hidden, but no less really there, not yet seen by the light of revealed truth, but still in the dawn of prefigurations. And what is fascinating to note is that her presence takes two different forms which correspond to the characters of the races in question. In China she is prefigured as a mother. The cult of motherhood is a special stamp of Chinese civilisation. I will quote what one Chinese girl student had to say:

> In a Chinese Christian, devotion to Mary takes the form of filial piety; our education accounts for this.

Remember the honour we give to parents. The mother has a very large share in this filial devotion. She has, therefore, special influence in the life of the family. And Chinese girls may well be shocked by the Protestant attitude to Mary. In China honour paid to anyone always rebounds on his mother. But Protestants seem to have no comprehension of this attitude; not only are they unaware of Christ's mother, but they actually seem to hate her being honoured. To me this seems against nature.

This cult of the mother is disposing China to come to Christ through Mary. It is through Our Lady as mother that China will receive the Gospel. And we may hope that a Christian China will deepen for us this mystery of the Blessed Virgin's motherhood by bringing to it the riches of its own teachings on motherhood, and that this will be an aspect of Christian dogma which it will help us also to understand more fully.

In India, on the other hand, it is the virgin who is honoured: throughout the history of this country, one can observe the homage paid to the virgin goddess, the cult of virginity. The Abbé Montchanin has expressed it magnificently in a work as yet unpublished:

Remotest Dravidian India adored virgins, women, mothers, fierce and gentle, cruel and tender, Kalis and Durgas. They have survived the centuries, the new layers of Aryan civilisation; they have remained at once cosmic and human, have become metaphysical : the material manifestation of the hidden God. In the concentration of the Yogin, they dance with a thousand arms, haloed with flame, or, like Shiva, with the wheel of Samsara. The *saktis* or consorts of the Buddhas, of the bodhisattvas, and even of those with no human shape, they are the dispensers of pleasure and death, the initiators into destruction, asceticism, and contemplation. They can be symbols of the void and of plenitude, of the one and the many, of being and non-being and that which is beyond both. In Sānkhya, the corresponding metaphysical category is Prakrti, or passivity, complementary to Purusa, that of activity. As contradictory as India herself, and as comprehensive as her religions, they stand at once for the wheel of becoming, with the double significance of movement and cessation, and the promise and foretaste of substanceless beatitude.

In Mary is the fulness of Virginity, of womanhood, of motherhood. Virgin from the beginning *et usque in aeternum*, she was prefigured by all that was virginal before her, and to her shall be united all virginity yet to be. The essence of her virginity is the singleness of her love. She was a perfect woman, attuned to God, fruitful through God and of God. She is Mother of the Word Incarnate, and her bearing of Him is more akin to the generation of that same Word by the Father than to the childbearing of ordinary human mothers. *Prius concepit mente.* Mother, then, of the Church, of mankind and of the world, she is the cosmic Mother, the universal Mediatrix, who initiates us into renunciation and bears in her gift the joy that never fades; who, like a dawn, heralds the irruption of God into the cycle of becoming. She is the vehicle of Christ and vessel of the Holy Spirit, the communicator of the Spirit who dwells within her in fulness and whose spouse she is, and of Christ in her eternal Motherhood; and by these two manifestations of the Father she calls the whole Church into His hidden life.

India, with its worship of goddesses, of virgins—the phenomenal aspects of Advaita—will respond to the human and cosmic grandeur of the Virgin Mary. Under the paradoxical images of the Canticle of Canticles—the dove and the army, *vox turturis, terribilis ut castrorum acies ordinata*—she appears as at once most sweet and most terrible; as mother and as woman she shows forth the God she bears, who slays and brings to life—*mortificat et vivificat*. . . . Surely India will be the country to find exactly the right sort of *hyperdulia* to answer that sweetness, that awe-inspiringness. It will see more and more deeply and fully the image of her in whom all times come together, who is the fulfilment of the work she herself began, who reflects the Origin, the Mediator, and the Spirit. This Virgin of Israel, this daughter of Abraham, is, above all, the sustainer of our contemplation of the Trinity, the prototype of the Church in its perfection, whose essence is to call on the Father—in whose paternity she has a temporal share—on the Son, whom she bears in His Kenosis and His entry into time—on the Holy Spirit, who through her overflows continuously onto mankind.

This text gives an excellent picture of how Christian realities were prefigured in the ancient world; this sort of aspiration towards the Blessed Virgin has gone up like a plaint throughout the centuries, and can never find its own answer. The idea of the Virgin is a glorious one, comprising both sweetness and sternness, as in Judith who was at once so gentle and so terrible. Her purity mirrors the holiness of God, and it is characteristic of purity to be at once the sweetest thing possible, and yet have a certain ruthlessness because love is as hard as death and as strong as hell. A heart fixed in love and virginity—which is singleness of love—admits of no division. Whence this extraordinary combination of sweetness and awe-fulness. If it is China who will deepen our understanding of Mary's motherhood, it is India who will discover to us the riches of her virginity.

And, lastly, we may say that what is true of the pagan peoples is also, in a sense, true of all mankind. It is not only the pagans who are living in Advent, for the whole Church is waiting in expectation of a fulness she has not known yet—though Christ is living and giving life in His Church, He is there in a hidden and mysterious way. His reign is not yet fully apparent to us in the glory of His royalty, and His dignity as Head of His Mystical Body. Therefore, in a sense, we are still living in the time before the true Church, before the heavenly Jerusalem, of which our Church as she is now is only a figure. There is an absence of Christ as well as a presence of Christ, and so there is also a special presence of Mary, inasmuch as it is she who prepared for the final coming of Christ. That is why her presence fills the space between Pentecost and the Day of Judgment, in exactly the same way as she filled the space between the Ascension and Pentecost. That great space in which we are now living is still a waiting time, still an Advent, still a preparation for the heavenly Jerusalem and the completion of the Church. We are still in shadow. The sacraments are shadows, the visible hierarchy is a figure of the heavenly banquet; Baptism is a figure of the final purification which will fit us to go into the glory of the Father.

That is why Mary has such an enormous place in the world and plays such a vital part there. It is she who is still at work within the Church preparing it for its final glory. What we are seeing in the Church is a gradual manifestation of Our Lady. We see it first through the successive dogmas by which her role is made clear to us, and since her receiving the title Theotokos—Mother of God—at Ephesus in the fifth century, the work she is doing has been becoming more and more visible to us— as, for example, in the middle of the nineteenth century, with her Immaculate Conception, and in our own day, with such mysteries as her mediation of all graces, or her Assumption. In all these dogmas, the mind of the Church is taking deeper hold of a spiritual reality it always possessed. The Church is, as it were, waking up to its consciousness of Mary, getting a clearer and clearer view of the reality of Our Lady, and the position Our Lady holds in her midst; that is why we are so distressed that our Protestant brethren cannot agree with us on this point, and show such hostility to our worship of Mary.

This manifestation of Mary is further expressed in Scripture's progressive revealing of her. Throughout the centuries the meditation of the saints has found it to contain more and more figures of her. Adam of Saint Victor wrote: "Thou wert chosen before the ages, thou hast long been hidden under the shell of the letter. Thou art the root from whom the flower of the world, Christ, was to spring. Solomon's throne, the veil of Gideon, the burning bush, all we believe to prefigure thee." The collective contemplation of the Church, put in writing in the liturgy sees Wisdom as a figure of her, saying, "Before the hills I was brought forth . . . playing in the world . . . with the children of men", sees her as the woman whose seed was to crush the serpent, Judith triumphing over God's enemies, Esther interceding for her people. The Eastern Church has shown us that she is the Spouse of the Canticle. And the newly composed Office of the Miraculous Medal shows us the woman in the desert in the Apocalypse, and the woman of the Lourdes apparitions, the woman crowned with twelve stars. Tradition has seen, and with good reason, in all of these, figures of the Church of the future. But bit by bit Christian contemplation has come to see them as incarnated in Mary.

The manifestation is still growing, and has been expressed by more frequent appearances of Our Lady in the past hundred years. One cannot but be struck by the furrow she drives right across the twentieth century, when human pride, based on scientific progress, seems to be pitting itself against God, and a feverish activity stirs the nations. Yet, still, outside the cities, in the solitude and peace of the mountains, in the sight of children, Mary appears, as if to remind us of the peace of God which man is powerless to break into. The Virgin of Lourdes, revealing to Saint Bernadette the hidden mystery of the Immaculate Conception, curing our bodies like the angel of Bethesda; the Virgin of la Salette recalling to us the holiness of Sunday, which is the mystical presence now of the kingdom of the future; the Virgin of Fatima, bringing closer to us than ever the call to prayer and penance; the Virgin of the Miraculous Medal, and the Virgin of Pontmain. Saint Grignon de Montfort declared that the last days of the world would be full of Mary's presence, and these apparitions do seem to be a sign of the perpetual imminence of the Last Coming, with their constant call to penance, which is the great message common to them all.

And while the visible signs of Mary's presence are growing thus clearer and clearer, in the inner, hidden world of sanctity it is becoming more and more evident that all the work of sanctification is done through a filial union with her "Fiat". And if she is the Mediatrix of all graces, because her mission is to form Christ in souls, and will be so while his world lasts, then her office is, above all, carried out in prayerful and contemplative souls. If holiness is God's action in forming the souls of those who give themselves completely to Him according to His will, one might say that every grace of holiness is a sharing in Mary's grace, for she gave her soul completely and utterly to Him. And if all holiness is produced by the Holy Spirit, then we may say that Mary's part becomes highly important in more and more ways, for upon her the Holy Spirit was always poured out, from the Incarnation: *Spiritus Domini superveniet in te*, until Pentecost: *Et erat mater Jesu ibi*.

There is a quite special relationship between the Holy Spirit and the Blessed Virgin. As I said earlier, Our Lady was first of all the one human being to recognise the Father and adore Him perfectly; and, secondly, she was the one human being to prepare for the coming of the Word, so that she directed all her energies to generating the Word in souls and in the Church. But equally she is, in a most mysterious way, the being the Church calls Spouse of the Holy Ghost, that is, she works upon mankind with the Holy Ghost to build the heavenly Jerusalem. Saint Louis Grignon de Montfort wrote that the reason why the Holy Ghost is not given to more in the Church nowadays is that Mary is not fully present. The Holy Ghost was given in abundance in the Upper Room, because Mary was there; at every time when Mary is present the Holy Ghost is poured out with abundance and produces the great works of God. For this reason there is much to be hoped from the emphasis on Mary in our century, that in the same measure as we turn towards such great mysteries as her Mediation and Assumption, God will, in His own mysterious way, prepare a new Descent of the

Holy Ghost, a new Pentecost. There again the presence of Mary is an earnest and a promise that the Holy Spirit is coming soon, that the infidels will be converted, and—I am most profoundly convinced—that there will be unity among Christians.

PART III

THE COSMIC MYSTERY OF THE
PASSION AND THE ASCENSION

I

THE MISSIONARY MEANING OF THE CROSS

An all-important aspect of the Cross which is far too often overlooked is its quality of universality. Christ, after speaking of the brazen serpent set up by Moses, said: "And I, when I shall be lifted up, will draw *all* things to myself." He was showing us that there is a relationship between the Cross and the drawing together of all things in Him. Saint Paul returned to this theme more than once in the letters he wrote when in prison, in passages of great mystery and richness. The best such passage is in the Epistle to the Ephesians, where Paul explains to us that Christ came to bring together the two separated races, the pagan Gentiles, that is, and the Jews, to break down the wall between them and bring all the nations into a single new race. What Saint Paul says of the pagan race and the Jewish race may also be applied to other races, so that Christian universalism, that is, the fact that all Christians are united in one body, is thus brought into relation with the blood of the Cross:

But now in Christ Jesus you, who sometime were afar off, are made nigh by the blood of Christ. For he is our peace, who hath made both one, and breaking down the middle wall of partition, the enmities in his flesh, making void the law of commandments contained in decrees; that he might make the two in himself into one new man, making peace; and might reconcile both to God in one body by the cross, killing the enmities in himself: and coming he preached peace to you that were

afar off, and peace to them that were nigh. For by him
we have both access by one Spirit unto the Father
(Eph. ii. 13–18).

This passage takes stock of the separation of the Jews
from the pagan nations, and the fact that up till then God's
message was reserved for the Jewish people, whereas
thenceforward all peoples were to be brought to know
the truth and live the life of the Spirit. And everything
that was said about the Jewish people in regard to the
pagans, can now equally be said of Christians in regard to
the non-Christian nations. It is far removed from God's
plan that those who first received Christ's message should
keep it to themselves, live within their own narrow limits,
and therefore set themselves up in a state of separation
from all other men; what He wants is that they should
become missionaries to help the others, that the unity
of all things in Christ be brought to realisation. The
divine economy moves forward, but does not change, and,
as we have just seen, what was once true of the Jewish
people in regard to pagan peoples is still true, but now of
Christian with regard to non-Christian peoples. This is
the tremendous mystery of how unity is brought about by
the Cross, that is, by nations renouncing their individual
privileges, for, simply put, the sin of the Jews was wanting
to remain *the* chosen people, and, therefore, refusing to
share their privileges with others. And what Christ stood
for was the end of this clinging of the Jews to a life within
their own narrow limits, and what came to replace it was a
charity that spread wide to all the nations.

During Mass this universalist aspect of the Cross is
symbolised when, at the Offertory, the priest, having
offered the host, uses it to trace a cross on the corporal,
as he says: *Pro totius mundi salute*—"For the salvation of

the whole world". By this gesture he somehow takes possession, in the name of the Cross, of the whole world, represented by the offerings before him, to consecrate it all to God, signing it with the sign of Christ. And what this sign of the cross, *pro totius mundi salute*, signifies is the cosmic nature of salvation: it indicates the four points of the compass, so as to embrace all nations, those of the north and of the south, of the east and of the west; they are the *totus mundus* for which the sacrifice of the Mass, the sacrifice of the Cross, is being offered.

If this symbol were isolated it might appear curious and incomprehensible, one might wonder whether the gesture could really have such a meaning; it is most interesting to see how often the Fathers of the Church studied this theme. There are some remarkable texts to the effect that the Cross represents the universalist nature of Christ's sacrifice in just this way. One of the finest is quoted by Père de Lubac at the end of his *Catholicisme*. It is very much to the point here. The text is called "The Cosmic Tree", and is by a second-century Father, Hippolytus of Rome:

This wood of the cross is mine for my eternal salvation. I am nourished by it, I feast on it, I am strengthened in its roots, I lie down under its branches, I fill my nostrils with its savour as with a sweet breeze. This tree, which stretches up to the sky, goes from earth to heaven. Immortal plant, it stands midway between heaven and earth, a strong prop for the universe, binding all things together, supporting the whole inhabited earth, a cosmic interlacing which embraces the whole motley of humanity; the Spirit holds it firm with invisible nails so that its contact with God may never be loosened, as it touches heaven with its peak, keeps its base firmly on the earth, and embraces all the atmosphere between with its measureless arms.

He was completely everywhere, in all things, yet there, alone and bare, He struggled against immaterial forces. When His cosmic battle came to an end, the heavens shook, the stars were near to falling, the sun was darkened for a time, stones were split open, and the world might well have perished, but Christ gave up His soul, saying: "Father, into thy hands I commend my spirit". And then, when He ascended, His divine spirit gave life and strength to the tottering world, and the whole universe became stable once more, as if the stretching out, the agony of the Cross, had in some way got into everything. Thou who art all in all, may thy spirit be in heaven, and thy soul in paradise, but may thy blood be on the earth.

In a somewhat earlier work of Saint Irenaeus, Bishop of Lyons, we find a similar text, which shows us that it was a theme dear to the Christian thought of the day:

Because He is the omnipotent Word of God, who in His invisible presence, is everywhere in the world at once, embraces the length and breadth, the height and depth, for it is through the Word that all things are ordered—because of this, the Son of God was crucified. Because of this, the Son of God was crucified, putting His imprint on the world in the form of a cross, in some way sealing the whole universe with the sign of the cross; and the sign of the cross, with its four dimensions, is the perfect sign that it is the *whole* universe that is so sealed. And indeed, it was necessary and fitting for Him, when He had become visible, to give the whole world a share in His universal cross, so that His visible operation should be made manifest under a visible form, for He is the One who makes the heights of heaven shine with what is born in the depths, under the earth, and stretches out to embrace the distance from east to west, and governs all the universe, calling creatures dispersed in every direction to a knowledge of the Father.[1]

It is worth noting this passage, where Irenaeus speaks of the length and breadth, the height and depth. For it calls to mind another text of Saint Paul, which I did not quote just now, also from the Epistle to the Ephesians (iii. 17-19), where Saint Paul says: "That Christ may dwell by faith in your hearts; that being rooted and founded in charity you may be able to comprehend with all saints what is the breadth, and length, and height, and depth; to know also the charity of Christ, which surpasseth all knowledge, that you may be filled unto all the fulness of God." Saint Irenaeus seems to have just the same idea as Saint Paul of the love of Christ filling the length and breadth and depth and height, embracing all mankind in charity; and this drawing in of all mankind is comparable to that deep-rooted tree by which here also all things are brought together. Christ's essential work is, in fact, to remake the unity of mankind. Christ is the new Man, who takes to Himself all of a man and all mankind. I think these are the two aspects under which Christ's work is seen in this perspective, and it is vital that we understand them.

First of all Christ draws to Himself all of a man. This brings us to the heart of one of the greatest problems of today. The Christian, following Christ, must resemble

[1] *Demonstration of Gospel Truth*, p. 46.

Him wholly; and the only way to do this is by the Cross. Now, the great temptation in the world today is—in trying to save man, wanting to do this more effectively and get better results faster—to sacrifice part of him, as if the weight of what is divine in him is too heavy for him to bear. They want to reject it, and bring all their efforts to bear on the temporal organisation of human life, to make a city to the measure of man reduced simply to his temporal desires, whence any suggestion of things eternal is barred.

And the temptation is very great. Mankind today gives the impression that Christianity is too heavy a weight for it. Such is our moment of history, such the position of Christians today. Christ said that He would return in a little while; this gave the early Christians the courage they needed to do the hard task set them. And now it looks as if we were being kept waiting for Christ's return, and though Christians go on proclaiming their certainty that He will return, men are getting tired of waiting for Him. And now, as Christ still has not come, they are tempted to take matters into their own hands, to get along without Him, to put all their hopes of saving their earthly city in their own efforts, their own methods.

A Christian faced with this attitude, which is the attitude of so many of our fellow-men, often finds himself in rather a painful predicament, somewhat at a loss. He wonders—quite rightly—whether his Christian principles do not impair his effectiveness to act in this temporal city, whether his scruples of conscience do not unfit him for the dishonest pledges, the acts of violence, which temporal action in the world calls for. He often finds himself forced to quit the fight because his conscience asks too much of him, and therefore he is less adapted to the struggle of the moment, and worldly efficiency.

He must recognise his true vocation: to refuse to allow man's destiny to be reduced to his temporal fulfilment, and to try and save what is eternal in him. He must see in all its depth what it means to be a man. He must be a man of contemplation, and if he is not that then he is not a Christian; if his deepest roots are not embedded in the world of the Trinity, if he does not try to penetrate its luminous obscurity, and, like Peter and James and John, set up his tabernacle on Mount Thabor, then he is no true Christian. Social, exterior action must not be allowed to take first place in our Christianity. We are called to share the intimate life of the divine Persons, and there will always be a part of us reserved for that. That is the full flowering of our deepest human dignity, and if you do not understand this you cannot call yourself a son of God, as many people today think they can and still claim that a Christian's first duty is to work for the improvement of the social order.

He must also see in all its *breadth* what it means to be a man: he must be a man of charity. Peter, James and John said: "It is good for us to be here, let us make here three tabernacles", and very soon the cloud disappeared, and they saw only Jesus, Jesus in His humanity; He was calling them from the contemplation of His divinity to the service of His humanity, called them therefore from contemplating the Blessed Trinity to the service of their brethren. Only Jesus—that is, Jesus as we see Him in our brothers, Jesus as He is now in His humanity, in all who suffer, in all who are ill, in all who are poor, in all whom it is our duty to serve by charity.

And that is the meaning of the Cross: at once the height and depth of contemplation, and the length and breadth of charity. It sinks into the depths of God and spreads out to the limits of mankind itself: it withdraws into contemplation of God, and at the same time embraces all men as brothers. That is why, every time we make the sign of the cross, we bring this to mind; when we raise our hand to our forehead in honouring the Father, it should remind us that we are called to contemplate the Father face to face, and when we move our hand from one shoulder to the other, we should be reminded that the charge of our brethren falls on our shoulders and that we are responsible for them.

That is the task—that the anguish—of being a Christian, and it is no wonder that many try to escape it, that it seems too heavy, that the burden of being a Christian seems more than they can bear. And the Christian knows that, by fulfilling this, not only does he save himself, but he is saving man from himself, defending man against himself, against that self which is trying to mutilate him, against that self which is trying to dash from his shoulders the cross he finds too heavy, and, with it, that part of himself which only God can satisfy. The Christian knows full well that what he is defending is manhood itself, that, by reminding man that he was made for God and for His Cross, he is reminding him of what it means to be a man.

Let us never try to simplify our life too much; that it is not simple is one of our reasons for being sure it is the truth. If a thing becomes too simple one may well wonder whether some essential part may not have been left out. We must accept our burden, even though we do not know how we can ever carry it; it is of the essence of a Christian's life that he never knows how he will manage to do anything, that of himself he is quite helpless, and must simply go forward in faith; he does not know where he is going, nor how, but simply that Christ is there, and He has the words of eternal life.

What is true of each one of us is also true of the Church

in the world today. It is exactly the same. Men are trying to force her to limit her action to temporal matters. The Church refuses. She wants to fulfil her whole purpose, and though mankind may reject her motherly care, she continues to watch over a sick humanity, bent upon serving it in its totality, and she knows that one day her charity will win over the resistance put up by men.

That is why she is not the least afraid. She does not fear persecutions, for she knows there is time yet. She lets mankind, still young perhaps, show its every feeling, the crises of its adolescence; she knows these crises will pass, and that these men will come back to her. The Christian's job is clear: simply to be Christian, to carry on with what he has to do, true to everything his Christianity asks of him, never watering it down, never afraid of being misunderstood or persecuted, knowing that his Master was persecuted before him, and knowing that it was by His Cross that He triumphed to save the world. The Cross was the greatest failure of all time: never has any cause seemed so thoroughly lost as when, on Good Friday, Jesus died on the Cross and His disciples were scattered, and yet that was the moment when mankind was saved—the very men who crucified Christ were made instruments of the world's salvation.

It is just the same with the Church today; let her be persecuted, crucified—what matters is that she remain faithful, and if she is faithful she will be crucified; by what seems to be failure she is often saving men. Those words of benediction will re-echo: "They shall look on him whom they pierced." They will look on her. That is something worth our remembering today: men will one day look upon her whom they crucified—they will start by crucifying the Church, and later they will look to her. They will see their ingratitude for what it is, they will turn to her seeing how empty they have made the world by their attempts to stop her work, for only she has the words of eternal life.

The second aspect of this unifying by the Cross is that Christ unites all men; Christ works out the unity of the world by His Passion, first interiorly, individually, in each man, then totally, universally. Here, too, the Church follows Christ, and her claim to be the unity of the world is one which shocks many people. They would like, on the contrary, to reduce the Church to a moment of history, or at least to be the product of a particular civilisation. They think the Church has had her day, that she corresponds to a certain period of the history of the world which is now past history. And yet the Church still goes on claiming that she alone can bring unity to the world, because only in her would the unity of man have any meaning, for she is founded on the fact of a single human family gathered round the Father, one in the Son. Beyond this there is *nothing* that can bring about human unity—here the mind of the Church sees very deep—for this is the only reality big enough to transcend all human divisions; such was Saint Paul's idea in the Epistle to the Galatians, when he said that Christ unites master and slave (class distinction and social warfare), that he unites man and woman (the drama of human love with all the divisions it makes), and, lastly, that he unites Jew and Greek (unity of the nations).[1] It is an extraordinary text, for it seems to apply quite exactly to all the problems of today, and it is most interesting that Saint Paul could describe as long ago as that the state of the world we are now living in. He tells us that it is by the blood of the cross of Christ that all these differences are overcome, and that in Christ there is neither

[1] See G. Fessard, *Esquisse du Mystère de l'Histoire*, Rech. Sc. Rel., 1948.

master nor slave, man nor woman, Jew nor Greek, but that all are one in Christ, that is to say, all belong to one race, the race of the sons of God, because all are one in His only-begotten Son.

So much for the specifically missionary aspect of the Cross. The mystery of the Cross means this: each nation, with its own characteristics, its own civilisation, must die to its arrogance, must give up all attempt to be the centre of the world, must submit to having its pride shattered; for it is only thus, by the Cross, that the nations can become fit to share in the greater unity of the Church, in which all are brought together in Christ.

This brings us up against the great obstacle to unity, and the reason why there is such a close connection between the Cross and unity: the greatest obstacle anyone can put to unity is to want to make himself the centre of things. We know this is so in our individual lives. In so far as we want to make a centre of ourselves, in so far, that is, as Christ is not the single centre of all things to us, we are setting ourselves up against Him. Now every nation naturally wants to be the centre: the world today shows this most clearly. There you have the carnal spirit let loose: each one wants to be the centre of the entire universe, and if any nation does want to bring unity to the world it is by gathering the rest round itself.

The Jews wanted all the nations to come and adore at Jerusalem, becoming, *ipso facto*, servants to the people of Israel. In the same way today a nation can be tempted to want dominion over all the others and think that that would be unity. Now such is not the meaning Christ attached to unity, nor is it the meaning the Church attaches to it. What they call unity results from a conversion, not from seizure or domination. It is a unity which is achieved by each one's living not for himself but for everyone, for all the others, when each really practises charity, which means, as Père de Montcheuil said, seeking perfect human fulfilment not only for oneself but for all other human beings, to sympathise with all that is good in the world, to will disinterestedly the good of all other creatures.

This, which holds good for individuals, holds good, too, for all mankind, and we are only working towards uniting the world in so far as we can love other nations without wanting to remake them in our image. We know how hard this is. We know that even in the Church herself there is a temptation to that kind of assimilation. We know how, in regard to the eastern Churches, the western Church has sometimes tried to effect a certain amount of Latinisation, and how such attempts have always been disastrous; we know still how hard it is for us to get outside ourselves enough to give full acceptance to a different mentality from our own, to give full acceptance to a Russian, or Hindu, or Chinese Christianity which would have a completely different physiognomy from ours in the unity of the one faith, never to try and impose our way of thinking on them.

And yet that is the very condition of unity: to respect the fundamental makeup of others is essential for unity in charity, which is quite different from unity produced by imperialism, or any sort of outside pressure. And this supposes the Cross. It supposes the giving up of individual egoism, imperialism, the will to impose oneself on others; it supposes instead the will to be the servant of others. Christ Himself made just this renunciation; the death of Christ was a symbol of the Jews as a whole dying to their privileges; it was a simple acceptance of the destruction of all that had gone before, so that the Gentiles could come into the Church, so that by His death, in some way, that seeking for their glory as a race, which had been the sin of the Jews, was blotted out by the humiliation of Christ. At that moment He was truly the Son of Man, as portrayed in the Book of Daniel, that is to say, as an incarnation of the whole Jewish community, dying in Him, to rise on the day of Resurrection as the universal man.

We may note, in concluding, one fact which gives the symbol of the cosmic Cross a quite special importance from a missionary point of view. In India we meet the notion of a cosmic tree, the symbol of a sort of universal axis planted in the centre of the world, which supports the sky, whose roots go deep into the earth, which in some way unites the whole world in itself. And it seems very likely that Hippolytus, in the text I quoted just now, was inspired by this Hindu thought of the cosmic tree. We know that the influence of India at that time in the Mediterranean world was considerable. In the Alexandria of the second and third centuries they knew a lot about India, and such pagan authors as Plotinus were greatly influenced by Hindu thought, as were such Christian authors as Clement of Alexandria. What Hippolytus was doing in that text was what we nowadays see as the way missionaries must go to work in India, trying, that is, to lay hold of every point of contact through which Christian ideas might be fitted into the representations, the cultural methods, and the ways of thought in India. We have here an effort to give men the first glimmer of a symbol for the mystery of the Cross, and of the Cross as a universal mystery. This is something similar to that strong and holy virgin so constantly found in Indian mythology, who is the first shadowy figure of the Virgin of the Canticle, likened to "an army with banners".

You see, then, that this page of Hippolytus takes on quite a new sort of missionary significance if this great Hindu theme of the cosmic tree becomes the best way of explaining the universalist character of the sacrifice of the Cross, and if we can only show India that, in this cosmic tree, what she has discovered is a mysterious prefiguration of the Cross.

And the Cross seen thus, inasmuch as it is the symbol, the sign of the drawing together of all things in Christ, inasmuch as it is the best of all missionary symbols, is seen under the aspect which will have the deepest, most hidden resonances for the Indian mind. Perhaps that is how we should first present the Cross to them, showing them how sacrifice is the only possible way to achieve this universalism which is their greatest desire—for syncretism is the one thing most sought after in India today— this unity of all things in a single religion. We must first show them the Cross, then Christ on the Cross; we must begin by showing them the huge, bare cross, and then show them that it has no meaning unless Christ is placed upon it, and that what makes it that cosmic tree, what makes it a universal Cross, is that it is not simply a bare piece of wood but the wood on which Christ hangs, with his blood running down it.

II

THE ASCENSION AND MISSIONARY EXPANSION

CHRISTIAN thought and piety have not gone very deeply into the study and understanding of the Ascension, though it is a mystery of immense richness. One is particularly struck by certain texts from Saint Paul in which he studies it in connection with the expansion of the Mystical Body— in other words, with the missionary problem. In other New Testament texts the same relationship is set up between the Ascension and the apostolate under its three chief aspects; the mission of the Holy Ghost in the world, the diversity of functions within the Mystical Body, the universality of the Spirit's working and the establishing of all things in Christ. A study of the most relevant of these texts will help to deepen our missionary spirituality.

We find, to begin with, two very notable texts in the Epistle to the Ephesians:

I, hearing of your faith in the Lord Jesus, and of your love towards all the saints, cease not to give thanks for you, making commemoration of you in my prayers, that the God of our Lord Jesus Christ, the Father of glory, may give unto you the spirit of wisdom and of revelation, in the knowledge of him: the eyes of your heart enlightened, that you may know what the hope is of his calling and what are the riches of the glory of his inheritance in the saints. And what is the exceeding greatness of his power towards us who believe, according to the might of the operation of his power which he wrought in Christ, raising him up from the dead, and setting him on his right hand in the heavenly places, above all principality and power and virtue and dominion, and every name that is named, not only in this world, but also in that which is to come. And he hath subjected all things under his feet, and hath made him head over all the Church which is his Body, and the fulness of him who is filled all in all" (i. 15–23).

All the grace in the Church, then, all the gifts of the Holy Spirit and the riches of eternal glory awaiting the saints, all this is the result of the victorious strength of Christ as shown in his Ascension. That is what Saint Paul is pointing to in those mysterious phrases, "above all . . . power", etc; and when he says, "every name that is named", he is opening up to us vistas of infinite spiritual worlds. On Ascension day the Father established Christ, the Incarnate Word, in His glory as supreme Head of the Church. On that day Christ became Head of the Mystical Body, and the Mystical Body is essentially a communication of the glory of the risen Christ to all mankind incorporated in it. The mystery of the Mystical Body was instituted at the Ascension, to be brought fully into effect at Pentecost.

In another text from this Epistle the Ascension is even more clearly indicated. It is one of the richest and most mysterious passages in Saint Paul, a text one could never weary of meditating and discussing:

Ascending on high, he led captivity captive; he gave gifts to men (Eph. iv. 8).

Christ has ascended on high—that is the Ascension. He

led captivity captive, setting man free from the powers of evil to whom he was captive, and henceforward God's gifts are showered plentifully on the world, grace begins to flow within the Mystical Body through the sacramental life. It is because Christ is present in the glory of the Father that the grace which is a sharing in His glory is continuously communicated to all of mankind incorporated with Him. Christ dwells within the Mystical Body as a living and lasting source of grace and holiness.

Saint Paul goes on: "Now that he ascended, what is it but because he also descended first into the lower parts of the earth?" What does the Passion mean but that Christ went down into the realm of death? This is a point that is seldom explained, and therefore we often fail to understand the significance of Christ's Passion for the whole world. Death is an evil power which, in company with sin, dominates mankind. Sin and death are two names for the same thing: death of the soul, and, resulting from it, death of the body. What was Christ doing in His Passion? Christ went down into death. He went where death is master. He put Himself into death's hands. The lower parts of the earth—the phrase does not simply mean the tomb, but also the lower regions, and in Greek theology the Resurrection was not simply Christ coming out of the tomb, but Christ coming up from hell. The notion is not the same—and the theological implications are far deeper. Christ went down into the domain of death, to that manhood which was under death's dominion, and there was a moment when death could cry "I am the victor". To which Saint Paul gave that magnificent answer: "Oh death, where is thy victory?" Death, whose name is Satan, thought on Good Friday to be forever victorious, for Christ Himself was its prisoner. And then, on Easter morning, the gates burst, the prisons of death were opened up: "O Death, where is thy victory?"

Christ could not conquer death in this particular way without first becoming its prisoner. He fell into its power to set mankind free. And this gives His death an incomparable realism, and an incomparable grandeur, and gives the word *Redemption* its fullest meaning. It was not simply a buying back, the squaring of an account between Christ and Satan, but Christ's struggle against the powers of evil, and His victory over them all and over the dominion of death. This explains the rites of baptism as practised in the Early Church. The descent into the baptismal pool, which Saint Paul connects with the burial of Christ, symbolised this going down into death. The newly baptised were incorporated into Christ's death before emerging victorious with Him. That victory of Christ's holds good for all men. Every man should reproduce in himself the whole mystery of Christ—His Passion, Resurrection, and Ascension—and baptism is a symbol of that conformity with Christ which is to be carried on throughout life. Christ's victory over the powers of evil is completed in us through mortification and the final liberation it brings.

Saint Paul continues, "He that descended is the same also that ascended above all the heavens, that he might fill all things." Christ has gone up above all the heavens, that is above every creature. You realise that to the Fathers of the Church the heavens and the angels were one and the same thing. When you meet either word, *cœli* or *angeli*, it may be replaced by the other. The heavens lend the angels their vastness; that is why it is quite wrong to picture angels as beings with wings, for they are immense spiritual worlds. To be raised above the angels is to be raised above that mysterious spiritual creation which surrounds us on all sides. We are immersed in the world of spiritual powers, both the bad, those princes of this world with whom Saint Paul tells us we are always in combat, and the good, those angels who surround the altar during Mass, whose presence is so profound and so real a thing that our human drama will always be played out in the background of this great spiritual drama. The Ascension also means that Christ's manhood was raised above the whole spiritual creation. It is an extraordinary thing that our needy human nature should be, in Christ, raised up above the angels who by nature are so much higher. One aspect of the mystery of the Ascension is the wonder of the angels at adoring the God-Man. According to certain Fathers of the Church, the sin of the angels was refusing to accept the Incarnation of the Word, because it raised mankind above them, which they found humiliating.

We must try not to picture Christ going up to heaven between two little angels. There were, of course, two angels who came to console the Apostles after the Ascension. "Two men stood by them in white garments. Who also said, Ye men of Galilee, why stand you looking up to heaven? This Jesus who is taken up from you into heaven, shall so come as you have seen him going into heaven." But the presence of these two was simply a visible manifestation of the legions of angels surrounding Christ, who watched Him in wonder as He went past their ranks to be raised to the glory of the Father, to lift mankind above all the spiritual worlds to that glory.

Saint Gregory of Nyssa gives us a most extraordinary description of Christ rising through the spheres of angels on the day of His Ascension, and the angels not recognising Him. *Quis est iste?*—Who is that?—they ask. . . . And the angels who are with Christ answer: *Rex gloriae ipse est, rex gloriae*—Yes, He is indeed the King of glory. The angels do not recognise the Word of God in this man with the traces of His Passion still upon Him. It is, however, the same King of glory they saw descending to earth when the Word took flesh, returning clothed with the same humanity but this time bruised by death, still bearing the wounds of the Cross.[1] This dialogue is the prelude to a heavenly liturgy of extraordinary grandeur, which expresses the central meaning of the Ascension, and Saint Paul orchestrates all its themes most admirably. He goes on to show us what follows from the mystery: "He has ascended above all the heavens that he might fill all things." Another extraordinary statement. It is only in so far as Christ has ascended above the heavens that He can fill all things. In other words, the grace which is in Him can, when He is lifted up above all creation, spread out to fill all creation. It fills human creation first of all, inasmuch as Christ is now the source of growth in the Mystical Body. But it also fills angelic creation, so that, as Saint Paul tells us, He may be first in all things, King of men, but also King of angels, *Rex angelorum*, so that the Word may rule a truly universal Kingdom. His kingship was instituted when He entered into glory; it will be established forever on the Last Day when Christ comes to take visible possession of His Kingdom. Till then, His victory is still going on in mankind, and also in the world of angels, where God is working mysteriously to "fill all things".

Saint Paul at once goes on to touch on another theme that concerns the apostolate: "And he gave some apostles, and some prophets, and other some evangelists, and other some pastors and doctors, for the perfecting of the saints, for the work of the ministry, for the edifying of the body

[1] *Three Eschatological Texts of Saint Gregory of Nyssa*, Rech. Sc. Rel., 1940.

of Christ." The fruit, therefore, of Christ's entry into His glory, is the *mission*, that is, the fact that men are chosen and called in Christ and in the Holy Spirit to do the work of evangelising, as apostles, prophets, pastors or doctors, so as to build up the body of Christ. It seems odd that Saint Paul does not speak of Pentecost—he goes straight from the Ascension to the mission—for we know that it was at Pentecost that the *charismata* were given, the spiritual gifts which turned some into prophets, others into apostles, or evangelists, because these are things effected by the working of the Holy Spirit. But what Saint Paul wants to make clear is that the Ascension was the cause of Pentecost. It was from the moment when Christ entered into the glory of the Father that His action became life-giving within the Church, and that He began to teach the Church through the Apostles, through those who gave themselves to Him to work for His Kingdom.

Let us now look at the descriptions of the Ascension in the Gospels: we shall see that Saint Paul's text gives them their fullest meaning. Christ said: "Go ye into the whole world, and preach the gospel to every creature . . . And the Lord Jesus, after he had spoken to them, was taken up into heaven, and sitteth on the right hand of God; but they, going forth, preached everywhere; the Lord working withal, and confirming the word with signs that followed" (Mark xvi. 15, 19–20).

Here, as in the Epistle to the Ephesians, the Apostles' mission is bound up with the Ascension. In Saint Mark's Gospel one might get the impression simply of two facts stated side by side; Saint Paul shows their organic relationship: it is Christ, risen into the glory of the Father who becomes the Source and the Head of the Mystical Body and orders its development: "the Lord working withal"— Christ acting in the Church as source of the Apostolate.

At the beginning of the Acts of the Apostles we have a further description of the Ascension which sets up the same bond between it and the spreading of the kingdom: it was after Jesus had said to His Apostles: "You are witnesses of these things", that He was lifted up from their sight. Saint John expresses the same mystery in a different way. During the discourse after the Last Supper Christ explained that it was necessary for Him to go to the Father, so that the Holy Spirit might come—"If I go not the Paraclete will not come to you" (John xvi. 7).

In the Epistle to the Hebrews we find another text about the Ascension, in a new perspective, that of the priesthood. The Epistle to the Hebrews is centred upon priesthood and sacrifice, showing sin as essentially man's refusal to recognise God's rule, and sacrifice as a recognition of it and therefore a means of returning to God's favour. By the Son's sacrifice mankind was brought back into communion with the Father. And the author expresses this in a text bearing directly on the Ascension: "Christ, being come an High Priest of the good things to come, by a greater and more perfect tabernacle, not made with hand, that is not of this creation: neither by the blood of goats, or of calves, but by his own blood, entered, once into the holy of holies, having obtained eternal redemption" (Heb. ix. 11 ff). It was at the Ascension that Christ entered into the true sanctuary, of which the Holy of Holies in the Temple was merely a figure, that is to say, into the Glory of the Father, having set man free from the slavery of sin and of death.

To the extent that the mystery of the Ascension is bound up with the idea of priesthood and sacrifice, it also is contained in the sacrifice of the Eucharist. After the consecration, the priest recalls not only the blessed Passion and Resurrection of Our Lord "but also his glorious Ascension"—*sed et in caelos gloriosae Ascensionis*. The whole mystery of Christ is there in the Mass, so the Ascension must be present. For a sacrifice to be complete, the victim must be offered—it must also be accepted. The Old Testament tells us of sacrifices that were not accepted, or at least not fully accepted, by God. The Ascension was Christ's sacrifice being accepted by the Father. It is by union with this sacrifice that ours is made effective, that God looks upon it with benevolence, that by it we are really in communion with God; that is the meaning of the Mass. The Ascension is actually represented, too, in the liturgy of the Mass, for it is the nature of a sacrament that the reality should be not merely signified but present. The priest prays to the Father that Christ should be presented by the hands of His holy angel on His altar on high: *in sublime altare tuum*. The Ascension is wonderfully evoked there. The Victim offered on the altar on high is Christ presenting Himself before His Father in heaven, bearing the wounds of His Passion and thereby drawing down the good pleasure of the Father on mankind.

In one of the most tremendous scenes in the Apocalypse the same mystery is again shown to us. Saint John sees a sealed book, whose seal cannot be broken, and the mystery is set before the whole heavenly world.

> And I saw a strong angel, proclaiming with a loud voice: Who is worthy to open the book and to loose the seals thereof? And no man was able, neither in heaven, nor on earth, nor under the earth, to open the book, nor to look on it. . . . And one of the ancients said to me: Weep not; behold the lion of the tribe of Juda, the root of David, hath prevailed to open the book . . . And I

saw, and behold in the midst of the throne, and of the four living creatures, and in the midst of the ancients, a Lamb standing, as it were slain (Apoc. v. 2–6).

How curious: a lion is announced, and it is a lamb that appears, and a lamb slain in sacrifice. The picture is overwhelming. Christ's victory is the victory not of a lion but of a lamb. Christ won the victory by sacrifice, and the vision of the Lamb breaking the seals signifies the Ascension. All creation, Saint Paul tells us, awaits redemption by the Son of God. To Saint Gregory of Nyssa, the whole angelic creation was in expectation, too. They are there, around God's throne, waiting until the book is at last unsealed—until the gates of death are burst open, and this cannot happen until the Lamb that was slain returns from the dead and receives from the right hand of Him who sits on the throne the book containing the names of the elect.

Thus often where the Ascension is not explicitly mentioned you still find allusion to it in some of the richest and most mysterious passages in Scripture. Notice, too, that at Mass the words describing the Father's acceptance of the Son's sacrifice are followed by a request that the Holy Ghost may come upon us "that we may be filled with every heavenly blessing and gift". The representation of the mystery of the Ascension is followed by that of Pentecost.

So much so that certain liturgists think that the prayer *Supplices te rogamus*, in the Mass, corresponds to what is known in the eastern liturgies as the epiclesis. In them the consecration is followed by a prayer to the Holy Ghost to descend upon the offerings and consecrate them. The Easterns think that the offerings are actually consecrated only by this epiclesis, which is one of the main points of difference between us. In our liturgy there is no epiclesis, and it is by the words of consecration that the bread and wine are changed. But the prayer *Supplices te rogamus* might be considered as a sort of epiclesis making a whole with the prayers of consecration; that would be a point of contact between us and the Easterns, for our liturgy is not substantially different from theirs. But to us the epiclesis is not so much the Holy Ghost descending upon the offerings as upon the congregation, for the fruit of consecrating the offerings is somehow a consecration of the community.

Now that we have put together so many texts from the Scriptures and the liturgy, we can see better the bond between the mystery of the Ascension and the mission of the Apostles. Saint Peter begins his epistle by telling us that the mission is a great mystery on which the angels are eager to gaze. The building up of God's Kingdom is a mysterious reality lasting from Pentecost to the Last Day, incomprehensible to the natural man; only grace can lead us to it.

The mission of today is threefold. It is, first of all, a mystery of *unity*. The Apostles were sent to the ends of the earth to teach all nations, because Christ, having risen to heaven, must be present in all creation. It is no more a question, as at the time of the old covenant, of God's taking one people in particular under His protection. The new mission, determined upon by God from all eternity, is to reconcile all things by Christ's blood *et omnia instaurare in Christo*. This mystery involves all mankind, and more than mankind, the whole spiritual universe.

In the second place, the mystery of the mission is the mystery of the missionary. Christ entrusted the spreading of His Kingdom to the Apostles, to those He had chosen as His tools in the work of evangelising. This vocation is a great mystery. It is clear that God could have communicated directly with each individual, yet He wanted His word to be handed on and His Kingdom to be spread by human intermediaries. He wanted us to have a share in saving the world and converting the nations, and the Apostles' mission is a direct continuation of the mission of the Word and the mission of the Holy Spirit. The mission of the Apostles is at once a single thing and a very diverse one. Holy Writ insists on the plurality of charismata; some are to be apostles, some prophets, evangelists, or teachers. The forms of the apostolate are many, but they are all one, because all get life from the same Spirit, all seek the same end. When missionaries cease to be united, then Christ is no longer with them. That is something worth thinking about. The reason why the evangelisation of the world is not further forward is because missionaries have not been faithful to charity. Opposition, rivalries, quarrels, jealousy, anything which weakens the unity of missionary work, stops it bearing fruit.

This unity in the diversity of functions is something Saint Paul insists on as of vital importance. Even then he felt the danger of a possible loss of charity threatening the work of the missions. We must, said Saint Bernard, put all the force of our action into our own vocation, but our charity must cover the whole world. He comments on that lovely phrase from the Canticle of Canticles: *Ordinavit in me caritatem.* He explains that in the order of action we must put our particular duty before everything else—do not let the contemplative try to do the apostle's work for him, nor the teacher try to care for the sick—but, he adds, "in our prayers we must put first what is most excellent in itself."[1] We must pray more for the most important interests of the Kingdom, even if they are not

[1] *Commentary on the Canticle,* xxvii, 10.

the ones we ourselves are engaged in. Charity will then become perfect in us, for it is proportioned to the reality of things, not to our personal point of view; selfishness will then be overcome at every moment. Outwardly we go humbly about our own work, inwardly we are working out the salvation of the whole world. We must be ready to be at once limited in our work and unlimited in the interior order of charity.

The true apostle loves in Christ everything good and beautiful that is done for the Kingdom of God. Saint Paul describes how "the whole body being compacted and fitly jointed together by what every joint supplieth, according to the operation in the measure of every part, maketh increase of the body unto the edifying of itself in charity" (Eph. iv. 16). That is a spirituality which would cover all of life. If each is faithful to the task allotted him, interior or exterior, each will contribute to the "increase of the body . . . in charity".

And the third and last aspect of the mission is that this work carried on in unity through the apostles proceeds from the *Holy Ghost*. It was He whom Christ first sent to the twelve, it is He who is always active in the Church animating the apostles. Among the gifts of the Holy Ghost there are some which are given us for our personal sanctification, but there are also some given freely to fit us for our work in building up the Kingdom of God. The gift given at Pentecost was this indwelling of the Holy Ghost in the Apostles, so that theirs was no merely human action, but the Spirit of Christ acting in and through His Apostles.

What matters, then, in an apostle is that he be an instrument united to God, *instrumentum conjunctum*, as Saint Ignatius said, for only in so far as He is united to God will the Holy Ghost act in him. He is not simply doing his own work, but Christ's, and he can do it only in so far as he is animated by the Spirit Christ sent and docile to His inspirations.

Too often we act in line with our own views, and our views are very narrow; only the Holy Spirit can enlarge our views to the measure of Christ's heart, and open up for us the great perspectives of God's plan. Then we shall see things as Christ sees them. It is the Spirit, too, who gives us strength, and the wisdom whereby we savour the things of God, that is to say, the increase of the Kingdom. For, at bottom, the only thing worth savouring is that— the growth of Christ in souls. This understanding and love of God's plan are not ours by nature, and only the Holy Ghost can give them to us.

We can see, then, how these three aspects of the mystery of the apostolate depend directly on the Ascension, or rather on Christ's entry into His glory. From that moment the Holy Ghost was able to work in mankind united in Him. As long as Christ had not entered His glory, mankind was, as it were, unlinked with the life of the Spirit. It was the Ascension that gave us the Holy Ghost. When Christ had become Head of the Mystical Body, had become the source of the government and sanctification of souls within the Church, He began to carry out the work of evangelising mankind, with those united to Him as His tools.

We are living in the midst of a great mystery which we must try to savour by contemplation, and to live by the apostolate: it is the mystery of evangelisation, it lasts from the Ascension to the Last Judgment—between the *Ascendit ad cælos* and the *Inde venturus est* of the Credo, between Christ's going up to the right hand of the Father, and His coming again at the end of time. This return will be heralded by an angel: "he shall so come as you have seen him going into heaven"; that is why the Apostles always looked towards the east when they prayed. A tremendous thing is happening—the conversion of the nations: let us meditate on this mystery and deepen our knowledge of it, and ask the Holy Ghost to make us grow in Him, and to make Him grow through us.

CONCLUSION

CHRIST's work is one thing, but no single phrase of ours can express its transcendence. That is why Scripture shows it under different headings, in different great categories, each of which appears in the Old Testament, attains fulness in Christ's human life, and is continued in the Church. Christ's work may be considered first as *priestly*, the offering of the perfect sacrifice which truly glorifies the Father, and which enables Creation to reach its goal. Under this aspect Christ's ministry fulfils the priestly figures of the Old Testament and is carried on in the priesthood of the Church. It may also be considered as a triumph over the power of the devil, over Death, Sin and Satan, whose captive, mankind, it set free. From this point of view Christ's ministry was *kingly*, fulfilling the messianic figures. And, lastly, it may be considered as a *prophetic* ministry. And this is the angle from which I propose to look at it now.

I had better first define exactly what I mean by the term *prophetic ministry*. A number of Protestant and rationalist authors start off with a definition of prophet that is primarily psychological, a man who presents what are commonly thought of as prophetic phenomena, such as trances and ecstasies. Therefore it must be noted that when I speak here of Christ as prophet I am speaking of a theological fact. C. K. Barrett[1] was quite right in saying that the word has two meanings. I am here using the word exactly as the Bible does, of a man whom the Holy Spirit introduces into the hidden designs of God so that he can be their witness till death. This may or may

[1] *The Holy Spirit and the Gospel Tradition*, London, 1947.

not be accompanied by ecstatic phenomena. G. Verbeke[1] has shown quite conclusively that inspiration, in the Hellenistic sense, which is caused by a quasi-material *pneuma*, and prophetic inspiration, in the Biblical sense, which is the *Pneuma hagion* taking hold of a man, have nothing in common necessarily, and have only been confused since Philo.

Often, too, people have far too narrow a conception of Christ's prophetic ministry, seeing it simply as His "predictions". It is because their whole notion of prophecy is falsely restricted. For prophecy is not simply one part of Christ's activity: it is one angle from which His whole work may be looked at. Saint John's seeing His miracles as bound up with His priestly ministry is just as right as Saint Luke's seeing them as *semeias*, figures, sacraments in the prophetic ministry: they are the *dynameis* which show the power of the Holy Spirit acting through the prophet. Saint Matthew and Saint Paul consider Christ's passion as a victory over the powers of evil and the setting up of God's Kingdom. But, as Martin Dibelius remarks,[2] Saint Luke shows it as the martyrdom of the Prophet. Prophecy, then, is one of the aspects under which we can see the whole mystery of Christ.

You see, then, that Christ's prophetic ministry is not confined to His teaching. Nor does the teaching solely stem from the prophecy. I am attaching a precise meaning to prophecy—the understanding and making known of God's view of history. Now only a part of Christ's teaching fits this definition. Christ was also the Legislator for God's Kingdom, and promulgated the charter for it. And this belongs rather to His kingly ministry, which is emphasised

---

[1] *L'Evolution de la doctrine du Pneuma du Stoicisme à St. Augustin*, 1945.
[2] *La signification religieuse des récits evangeliques de la Passion*, Rev. Hist. Phil. Rel., 1933.

in Saint Matthew's Gospel. Yet another work of His is to
reveal the Father, to bring to our knowledge the intimate
life of God. This is the aspect most clearly shown in Saint
John's Gospel. It may be linked up with the prophetic
ministry inasmuch as the Prophet is God's witness among
men. However, we will concentrate on what is strictly
prophetic, what bears on God's action in history.

After Malachy, there was no prophecy in Israel. That
fact is one of the strangest in the Old Testament. The
Jews constantly expected its return. The stones of the
altar of holocausts, which had been destroyed because
the Gentiles had profaned it, were put away in a safe
place "till there should come a prophet and give answer
concerning them" (1 Macc. iv. 46). Simon Maccabeus
was given the authority of high priest and leader of the
people "till there should arise a faithful prophet" (1 Macc.
xiv. 41). It is clear that the Jewish people considered that
the promise to Moses of a Prophet with a mission equal
to his (Deut. xviii. 15–19) had not been fulfilled by any
of the prophets during the time of the Kings, and that
they were still waiting for that Prophet to come. The
Gospel gives us an echo of this expectancy in the Jews of
the time. While John the Baptist was carrying out his
work the Jews sent to him priests and Levites to ask
him: "Art thou Elias? . . . Are thou the Prophet?"
(John i. 21). And the Jews, confronted with the tremendous works of Christ, are described as saying "some that
thou art Elias, others Jeremias or one of the prophets"
(Matt. xvi. 14).

From this last passage we must gather that Christ
seemed to the Jews to present the characteristics of a
prophet. And he was described as such both by Himself
and by His disciples. When the crowds gave Him the
title He made no protest: "And the people said, This is

Jesus the prophet from Nazareth of Galilee" (Matt. xxi. 11. Cf. Mark vi. 15; Luke vii. 16, xxiv. 19). He gave Himself the title: "A prophet is not without honour save in his own country and in his own house" (Matt. xiii. 57), and again: "I must walk today and tomorrow and the day following: because it cannot be that a prophet perish out of Jerusalem" (Luke xiii. 33). Immediately after the Resurrection the disciples on the road to Emmaus were speaking "concerning Jesus of Nazareth, who was a prophet mighty in work and word before God and all the people" (Luke xxiv. 19). I will come back to that remarkable expression. And Saint Peter, in his turn, speaking to the Jews after the Resurrection, shows them that Christ was the Prophet foretold by Moses and all the prophets, "from Samuel and afterwards" (Acts iii. 22–4). Thus Christ appears to fulfil every prophecy, both in the obvious sense that it was He that was prophesied, and also inasmuch as it prefigured Him, that is to say, inasmuch as He was Himself most eminently a Prophet, possessing the fullness of every prophetic attribute. I say "eminently", for although Christ was a continuation of the long line of prophets He went far beyond it. What He said of John the Baptist—that he was more than a prophet—is supremely true of Himself (Matt. xi. 9).

Not only does the New Testament give Christ the title of Prophet, but it also presents Him in action as one. This brings us to a most remarkable fact, which has been very much stressed by P. Dabeck in an article in *Biblica*.[1] The fact is this: whereas in Matthew's Gospel Christ appears as another Moses, the legislator of the New Law, in Luke's Gospel, on the other hand, He appears as another Elias. Dabeck has established this thesis with a great many parallels which seem quite decisive. It must

[1] *Siehe es Erschienen Moses und Elias*, 1942.

first be noted that Luke's Gospel is the Gospel of the Holy Ghost. His essential idea is to show Christ's life, and later on in the Acts the Church's life, as a continuation of the great works done by the Spirit in the Old Testament, since sacred history is the history of those great works, those *thaumata*, in three successive economies. As the Holy Spirit was the principle of the first creation, *moving upon the face of the waters* (Gen. i. 2), so it is clearly He who is alluded to as *coming upon* and *overshadowing* Mary at the Annunciation to initiate the second creation (Luke i. 35). And, by a further outpouring of the Holy Ghost, Pentecost was to inaugurate the third stage of God's plan. The rest of Luke's Gospel, followed by the Acts, shows us the Holy Spirit ordering events. It was He who led Jesus into the desert (Luke iv. 1). Peter was "filled with the Holy Ghost" when he spoke to the elders of the people (Acts iv. 8). Stephen argued with the Jews so that "they were not able to resist the wisdom and the spirit that spoke" (Acts vi. 10).

Now it belongs to the prophet to be introduced by the Spirit into the depths of God's designs, which only the Spirit can plumb, so that he will be their witness and instrument among men.[1] Such a one was Elias in the Old Testament; such, as Saint Luke saw Him, Christ in the New. There are more allusions to Elias in his Gospel than in the others. At the beginning we see John the Baptist going before Him "in the spirit and power of Elias" (i. 17). And Christ is compared to him even more closely. In the fourth chapter Christ points out an

[1] "In that same hour he rejoiced in the Holy Ghost and said: I confess to thee, O Father, Lord of heaven and earth, because thou hast hidden these things from the wise and prudent and hast revealed them to little ones. . . . All things are delivered to me by my Father . . . many prophets and kings have desired to see the things that you see and have not seen them" (Luke x. 21-4). It is interesting to note that the parallel passage in Matthew (xi. 25) does not mention the Holy Ghost.

essential characteristic of a prophet, to be rejected by his own people, and compares Himself to Elias: "No prophet is accepted in his own country. . . . There were many widows in the days of Elias in Israel . . . and to none of them was Elias sent" (iv. 25–6). As Elias brought the son of the widow of Sarepta back to life, so Jesus brought the son of the widow of Naim (vii. 11 ff.), and Luke is the only one to recount the incident. It is clear that what he tells is from a wish to connect Christ and Elias, especially since he notes the reaction of the crowd: "And there came a fear on them all, and they glorified God, saying: A great prophet is risen up among us" (vii. 16). And the Church, in bringing together these two episodes in the Lenten liturgy, is doing precisely what the evangelist intended.[1]

There are other marks of the literary dependence of Luke's Gospel on the Books of Kings. To a man who wanted to follow Jesus, and asked only first to say good-bye to his family, He answered: "No man, having put his hand to the plough, and looking back, is fit for the kingdom of God." This answer is reminiscent of what Elias said to Eliseus upon his making the same request— "Let me, I pray thee, kiss my father and my mother, and then I will follow thee,"—when Elias came upon him ploughing (3 Kings xix. 20). In both passages we find the same demand for immediate fidelity to a vocation. Elias brought down fire from heaven three times (3 Kings xviii. 38; 4 Kings i. 10, 12). Jesus upbraids His disciples for wanting to do the same (ix. 54); He said of Himself, "I am come to cast fire on the earth" (xii. 49), but it was a different fire, the Holy Ghost Himself, of whom Elias' fire was only the figure. These two incidents which

---

[1] Elias' appearance at the Transfiguration now becomes clear to us (Luke ix. 30).

bring Elias so vividly to mind come in a very crucial passage of Saint Luke's Gospel, that describing Christ's last journey to Jerusalem as He went to His Passion. It begins with these most solemn words: "And it came to pass, when the days of his assumption (*analempsis*) were accomplishing, that he steadfastly set his face to go to Jerusalem" (ix. 51). Now the chapter in the Book of Kings describing Elias' last journey, which was to end in his ascension (*anagein*), starts off with a similar passage. Saint Luke's expression *analempsis*, ascension, to describe the object of Christ's journey is an allusion to the ascension of Elias. And, too, it is noteworthy that the Ascension of Christ figures largely in Saint Luke, for he describes it twice (xxiv. 51; Acts i. 9), and that his "ascension" is the most striking part of Elias' story. And note that just before His Ascension, Christ gave His disciples the same command as Elias gave Eliseus, to wait there until they had received what God had promised (Acts i. 4; 4 Kings ii. 2).[1]

Thus the Gospel shows Christ as a Prophet. What does the designation mean, and what aspect of Christ fits it? To see this we must start off from the Biblical conception of the world. It is a carrying out in time of a hidden plan of God's, the *mysterium* spoken of by Paul. Sacred history is thus the history of the mighty works of God— the *gesta Dei*, the *mirabilia*—performed in time by the Holy Spirit. According to Genesis, the creation was the first of these great works. And, according to the writings of the prophets, the resurrection on the Last Day will be a new creation by the same Spirit. Christian revelation tells us of another work of the Holy Spirit, falling between the two, the Incarnation. And the Incarnation was followed by Pentecost, which was again an outpouring

[1] For further comparisons see Dabeck, *ibid*.

of the Holy Ghost. As well as these major works, sacred history is punctuated by other works of God—the great events of the Old Testament, especially the coming out of Egypt, Christ's miracles, and supreme among them the Resurrection, and, lastly, the sacraments of the Church.[1] In fact, one may say that the Exodus from Egypt, Christ's Resurrection and Christian baptism follow in perfect sequence, as three great works of liberation performed by the power of the Holy Ghost, corresponding to the three great stages of world history.

The Biblical notion of a prophet can be completely defined in relation to this perspective. A prophet is one who has been given an understanding of history by the Holy Spirit who is its Author. That is why Christ's prophetic ministry began when He received the Holy Ghost on the day He was baptised: "Heaven was opened, and the Holy Ghost descended in a bodily shape as a dove upon Him" (Luke iii. 22). The dove here recalls the Spirit brooding like a bird over the waters at the beginning of creation (Gen. i. 2). In the same way He produces a new creation in the waters of the Jordan. This creation was the inauguration of the preaching of the Word, of the Gospel, which is continued in the Church by the power of the same Spirit which came down upon the Apostles at Pentecost, and is still inspiring the preaching of the Gospel. Notice that each of Christ's major ministries was inaugurated by a manifestation of the Trinity: the public ministry at His baptism, the priestly ministry at the Transfiguration[2] in which the cloud symbolised the Holy Ghost, and the kingly ministry at the Ascension, when the cloud figures again. And we see that the two first theophanies were each followed by

[1] See Cullmann, *Urchristentum und Gottesdienst.*
[2] See, in this connection, Serge Boulghakov, *Of the Word Incarnate.*

a temptation—the first, the temptation in the desert, after His baptism, and the second when Satan tempted Christ through Peter, after His Transfiguration. It is thus clear what great solemnity attended the setting up of Christ's prophetic ministry, so that it was similar to the solemn calling of the ancient prophets and of the New Testament Apostles.

That Spirit who descended upon Christ at His baptism was to guide Him throughout His prophetic ministry. "And Jesus being full of the Holy Ghost, returned from the Jordan and was led by the Spirit into the desert" (Luke iv. 1). His meeting with John the Baptist was an exalted moment in the history of prophecy: the prophecy of the Old Testament summed up finally in John the Baptist, saluted the advent of the Prophet of prophets, of whom all the earlier prophecy was only the figure. And when we see Christ led by the Spirit into the desert, we cannot fail to remember Elias, led to the brook Carith after he had been called, and fed by ravens who brought him bread and meat morning and evening (3 Kings xvii. 3–6). Then, after His time in the desert, it was again under the influence of the Holy Spirit that Jesus began His prophetic ministry: "And Jesus returned in the power of the Spirit into Galilee" (Luke iv. 14). And when he was in the synagogue of Nazareth He proclaimed Himself the Prophet filled with the Holy Spirit—the Prophet foretold by the earlier prophets: "The Spirit of the Lord is upon me, wherefore he hath anointed me to preach the gospel" (Luke iv. 18; cf. Isa. lxi. 1–2). It was by the Spirit of God that He cast out devils (Matt. xii. 28). In his book *Der Herr*, Romano Guardini saw this outpouring of the Holy Spirit most clearly in the beginnings of Christ's prophetic ministry, bringing to mind both the first spring of creation and Pentecost: "The fulness of the Spirit was upon Christ as He came down from His baptism. It flowed over Him, and blossomed round Him. The Spirit wanted to act and speak, to express Itself in works and words."

This was indeed the same as the action of the Holy Spirit upon the prophets of the Old Testament. But it was also something quite different, in the first place because it was the fulness of the Spirit, whom the prophets of old had received only in part, wholly concentrated in Christ. "Your prophets," said Justin to Trypho, "each received from God one or other of these powers; and they acted as the Scriptures describe. Solomon had the spirit of wisdom, Daniel the spirit of understanding and counsel, Moses that of fortitude and piety, Elias that of fear, Isaias that of knowledge. Each had one power, or perhaps two, each in turn. The Holy Ghost rested, that is to say ceased, when He came after whom you were to receive these things no more; but in Him the gift, which, by the grace of the Spirit's power, He gives those who grow in Him, was to go on acting as had been prophesied."[1] Thus the gift of the Spirit showed itself in three successive outpourings: divided up among the Prophets, gathered together in Christ, and communicated by Him to His chosen ones.[2] Jesus is also united to the Spirit in the life of the Trinity. Therefore His possession of the Holy Spirit was not simply a gift of the moment, but His in permanence. And in Him this gift was given to mankind to be theirs forever. But from this Spirit, which is in Him and is His, flow His communications to humanity which is also His, and this is really one of those infinitely mysterious communications which the prophetic ministry manifests to us. It is in this sense that the coming of the Holy Ghost in the ancient prophets prefigured His coming in Christ

[1] *Dial.* 87, 4-8.
[2] *The Salvation of the Nations.*

who is the reality of Prophecy. Just as Christ's entry into the Temple of heaven at once fulfilled and did away with the priesthood of the Old Testament, so His mission of explaining and carrying out the divine plan at once fulfilled and did away with the Old Testament prophecy.

The Holy Ghost's purpose in inspiring the prophet is to make him a witness and an agent of the carrying out of God's plan in history. The Spirit of prophecy is, first and foremost, the Spirit of Understanding. Only the Holy Spirit can plumb the depths of God, and it is only He who gives the prophet access to them. But this understanding He gives is not simply a knowledge of God, it is also an understanding of God's plan. The prophet is, as it were, admitted into the confidence of the Trinity, and contemplates the unfolding of Its designs. He sees beyond the mere appearances of history, into the sphere of the sacred, that is to say, into the very reality of history, irrevocably made to be so by God. This history, to which he must give witness among men, he first gets as an object of contemplation. And his contemplation bears equally on the past, present and future. The prophets witness to the creation of the world, the judgment of water in the Flood, the covenant with Abraham, and God's power setting His people free from the Egyptian captivity, just as much as to the second creation of the new heavens, and the final covenant to be inscribed upon hearts of flesh, to the second exodus and perfect liberation.[1] Thus, the object of the prophet's contemplation is to see how all God's ways work together in history; and his purpose is, by witnessing to these ways of God, to lead men to give up their own ways and fit in with God's. On the threshold of the New Testament, Our Lady, contemplating the great works done by God, cried out her admiration in words that resound down

[1] See A. G. Hebert, *The Authority of the Scriptures*, 1947.

the centuries as the absolute expression of prophetic contemplation: "He that is mighty hath done great things. . . !"

But clearly the greater stress is laid on the things yet to come. That is the history of which Jesus is *the* witness. His preaching is always given in the light of the Last Day. He was not only teaching a doctrine; He was also fore-telling events for which men must prepare. Those events are the *Kairoi*, the decisive moments which "the Father hath put in his own power" (Acts i. 7). The first such event was His own Passion, which was, properly speaking, His hour (*Kairos*): "The days will come when the bride-groom shall be taken away from them" (Mark ii. 20). That was the first step towards the events at the end. I do not understand how Guardini, in *Der Herr*, can see Our Lord's first preaching as unconnected with the fact of the Passion, when the Passion, the Victory over death, was what He had come for. It was not an accident, but an essential part of God's plan. All the prophecy that came before foretold it. It is one of the mysteries of sacred history, which, like all God's plan, is hidden from carnal-minded men and revealed to little ones: "And he taught his disciples and said to them: The Son of Man shall be betrayed into the hands of men, and they shall kill him; and after that he is killed, he shall rise again the third day. But they understood not the word and they were afraid to ask him" (Mark ix. 30). It is characteristic of prophecy for men to refuse to understand it, because God's ways are utterly opposed to their own carnal ones. Mary of Bethany was the only one to grasp this mystery: "She is come be-forehand to anoint my body for the burial" (Mark xiv. 8). Jesus saw this mystery of the Passion in an apocalyptic setting as the central action in the cosmic struggle between Himself and the prince of this world, which began with the world's creation, and will end only on Judgment Day. It was certainly as a "seer" that He said: "I saw Satan like lightning falling from heaven" (Luke x. 18). And it was immediately afterwards that, Saint Luke tells us, "he rejoiced in the Holy Ghost" (x. 21). It is a mark of the prophetic Spirit to see all the cosmic repercussions and significance of a thing, to see it as part of the spiritual drama of history.

What Christ goes on to contemplate are the *Kairoi*, the decisive events, of the Church. The first is the denial of the Jews, and the coming in of the Gentiles, that supreme historical mystery, prefigured throughout the Old Testament by the substitution of younger sons for elder. "Many shall come from the east and west and shall sit down with Abraham, and Isaac, and Jacob, in the kingdom of heaven. But the children of the kingdom shall be cast out into the exterior darkness" (Matt. viii. 11–12).[1] Then came what Christ Himself called the "mysteries of the kingdom" (Matt. xiii. 11), which it was given only to His disciples to know. All Christ's preaching was an anouncement that the Kingdom of God was at hand (Matt. iv. 17). He revealed the mysteries of this Kingdom in parables, "I will utter things hidden from the foundation of the world" (Matt. xiii. 35). The Kingdom was a hidden one, present but invisible (Luke xvii. 20). It was gradual of development, like a grain of mustard seed (Matt. xiii. 32). It was a Kingdom whose subjects belonged to it only of their own free choice. The Apostles, who carried on Christ's prophetic work by their mission, that mystery upon which ". . . the angels desire to look" (1 Pet. i. 12), were to be filled with His Spirit. By some they would be welcomed: "He that receiveth you receiveth me. . . . He that receiveth a prophet in the name of a prophet shall receive

[1] This was the mystery of which Saint Paul was to be the herald (Eph. iii).

the reward of a prophet" (Matt. x. 40–1). But others would persecute them as they had persecuted all the prophets since the creation of the world (Matt. xxiii. 34).

When their mission was over, there would follow the final stage, the ultimate *Kairos*, the Judgment: "And this gospel of the kingdom shall be preached in the whole world . . . and then shall the consummation come" (Matt. xxiv. 14). The announcement of the coming Judgment dominated all Christ's preaching, as it had dominated the preaching of the prophets: "It shall be more tolerable for the land of Sodom and Gomorrha in the day of judgment than for that city" (Matt. x. 15). "The men of Ninive shall rise in judgment with this generation, and shall condemn it" (Matt. xii. 41). The parables largely related to the Last Day: "Even as cockle therefore is gathered together and burned with fire; so shall it be at the end of the world. The Son of Man shall send forth his angels, and they shall gather out of his kingdom all scandals, and them that work iniquity; and shall cast them into the furnace of fire" (Matt. xiii. 40–2). And that last great description of the Judgment gives more detail about the whole picture. There Christ's gaze takes in all future history: first, what was soon to happen —persecution of the disciples by the Jews, and the fall of Jerusalem—and then in the more distant future, the long wait during which the patience of many would flag, but the perseverance of the rest would triumph (Matt. xxiv. 12–13): and the period between the two was to be filled by the Church's mission. And lastly, in a great apocalyptic sweep, which recalls His seeing "Satan falling like lightning from heaven", Christ contemplates the coming of the Son of Man "as lightning cometh out of the east and appeareth even into the west" (Matt. xxiv. 27). Such are the perspectives of the Judgment: the cosmic upheavals, when "the powers of heaven shall be moved", which must in some way be bound up with the final overthrow of the "princes of this world". "And then shall appear the sign of the Son of Man in heaven." And "he shall send his angels with a trumpet and a great voice and they shall gather together his elect from the four winds" (xxiv. 30–1)[1].

This is the sacred history Christ bore witness to. His mission was to give evidence before men of God's ways, so that they might be converted, do penance, and give up their own ways. The prophets of old had already borne witness to this history. But here again, while Jesus continued their work, He went far beyond them. While His prophetic knowledge, as such, bore on matters proper to prophecy—on the nature of future events, and not their exact dates, which belongs to a different science—He never acted as a man to whom this knowledge had been revealed, but always as one who possessed it by right of nature, inasmuch as it was the Father's secret, and the Father had given all things into the hands of the Son. That is why Christ spoke with more authority than all the prophets: "Never did man speak like this man" (John vii. 46): for, first, Jesus spoke on His own authority, "not as the scribes"; and second, He was not only the prophet but also the object of the prophecy. He Himself was the reality of this sacred history to which He gave witness, because He fulfilled it in Himself, because it was He who had been foretold by the prophets of old and it was to His coming in glory on the Last Day that His own prophecy related. That is why He did not simply ask belief in His word, but in Himself, for He was Himself the Origin and End of history.

[1] On all of this see Léonce de Grandmaison, *Jesus Christ*, vol. ii: "Christ as Prophet".

To be a prophet means not simply to give witness to divine history but also to be the instrument of its accomplishment. Jesus was a Prophet, mighty in *works* and in words (Luke xxiv. 19). It is noteworthy that it was generally as a result of His miracles that the crowds gave Christ the title of Prophet: after raising the son of the widow of Naim (Luke vii. 16); after multiplying the loaves (John vi. 14); after curing the man born blind (John ix. 17). In point of fact, the prophet of the Old Testament performed works of power by virtue of the Spirit who was in him. Moses, Elias and Eliseus all did so. Now this power of action belonged supremely to Christ. It is instructive to compare Elias' laborious raising to life of the widow of Sarepta's son with Christ's absolute authority in commanding the widow of Naim's son to rise. And Peter was later to give the same command to Tabitha (Acts ix. 40). These three miracles which have so much in common point up the unity of the three economies. Above all, Christ's own miracles were only prefigurations of His greatest miracle of all, the Resurrection, when the omnipotence of Christ the Prophet is shown acting in the fulness of the divine power that is His by nature. Thus miracles, in that they are evidence of the Spirit's power acting in the prophet, are related closely to the prophetic ministry.

One final characteristic of the Biblical notion of prophet must be mentioned—persecution. It is a thing which seems to be absolutely of the essence of a prophet, of being the witness and instrument of God's ways. Men want to arrange history to fit in with their limited earthly vision, which is quite different from God's view of things. The prophet, therefore, who represents God's outlook, cuts across the plans men are making; and that is why they reject him. The conflict between the powerful of this world and the prophets, which fills the Old Testament, manifests the conflict between the two histories. There is no point upon which Christ more expressly established a continuity between Himself and the Old Testament prophets: "Woe to you, scribes and Pharisees, hypocrites! that build the sepulchres of the prophets, and adorn the monuments of the just, and say: If we had been in the days of our fathers we would not have been partakers with them in the blood of the prophets. Wherefore you are witnesses against yourselves, that you are the sons of them that killed the prophets. Fill ye up then the measure of your fathers" (Matt. xxiii. 29–32). You could hardly show more clearly that the Passion is the peak, the quintessence, of the persecution which had attached to prophets from the very beginning. Jesus warned His disciples that they would be equally persecuted, and so showed them that, like Him, they were carrying on the continuity of the prophets of old as witnesses of the ways of God: "Therefore, behold I send to you prophets, and wise men, and scribes; and some of them you will put to death and crucify; . . . that upon you may come all the just blood shed upon the earth, from the blood of Abel the just even unto the blood of Zacharias the son of Barachias, whom you killed between the temple and the altar" (Matt. xxiii. 34–5. See Luke xi. 50, where he speaks of "the blood of *all the prophets* which was shed from the foundation of the world").

Here the idea of "prophets" is linked up with that of "martyrs"—both as witnesses. They are found together even in the Old Testament, for even there the prophets were persecuted. Jezabel pursued Elias to put him to death (3 Kings xix. 2). This aspect of prophecy had been particularly stressed at the time of the Maccabees, when it often cost faithful Jews their lives to give witness of God.

That is where we find such stories as that of Isaias being sawn in two (*Ascension of Isaias*, v. 12). Tertullian alludes to this and recalls several instances of persecuted prophets when he writes: "Elias was pursued, Jeremias stoned, and Isaias cut in two."[1] Stories of the martyrdom of prophets were a regular literary form in pre-Christian Judaism. It seems as though Saint Luke had this literary form in mind when giving his account of the Passion. Martin Dibelius noticed this: "Judaism was already familiar with edifying stories of martyrdom; the story of the heroes and the persecution under Antiochus Epiphanes in the Book of the Maccabees is one example. Early Christianity also had its stories of martyrdom. The author of the Third Gospel gives us in the *Acts* an account of the first Christian martyr, Saint Stephen. It is easy to understand why he strikes similar notes in his account of the Passion."[2] Dibelius points out in particular the consoling angel and the sweat of blood in the agony, the words of consolation He spoke to the daughters of Jerusalem, His promise to the good thief that he should go straight to heaven—which was a privilege reserved to martyrs, His commending His soul into the hands of His Father. And later Christian stories of martyrdom make a point of stressing every possible parallel with the Passion of Christ.[3] What particularly stand out are any prophetic manifestations, especially the visions which accompanied most martyrdoms in the early centuries.[4]

In the religious reality of prophecy, then, everything is finally brought home to the great works of power performed by the Holy Ghost. The prophet is a man whom

[1] P. L. ii, 37.
[2] *Récits evangeliques de la Passion et leur signification religieuse*, Rev. Hist. Phil Rel., 1933.
[3] *Martyrdom of Polycarp*, i, 1; vi, 2.
[4] *ibid.*, v, 2; *Act. Perp. et Fel.*, x, 4 ff.

the Holy Spirit takes hold of to associate him with His action upon the world. Sacred history is entirely the work of the Holy Spirit. The prophets and their successors, the apostles, are instruments whom the Holy Ghost has lifted out of their natural setting to let them into the secret of God's plans for the world, and to make them witnesses of those plans in word and deed. They are so completely at one with God's view of things that they are necessarily in conflict with materialistic men who stand for this world's view of things. And this tremendous reality of prophecy culminated in Christ, the perfect example of it.

Now the Church, in the variety of her vocations, reproduces and carries on the various ministries of Christ, in His works of mercy and in His works of teaching, in His priestly ministry and in His kingly ministry. And each of these works is at once a Way to holiness and a function of the Mystical Body. We may well wonder here whether the prophetic ministry is not the model and pattern of that way to holiness in the Church today which is the apostolic life. The question of the apostolic way to holiness has for a long time been clouded by the idea we have inherited from the Greeks that *theoria* and *praxis* are opposed to each other, the former being superior, introducing us into the world of intelligible realities, whereas the latter leaves us in the world of appearances. But the Christian reality is the very dogma which the Greeks found it so hard to accept—the Incarnation, the doctrine of a divine and divinising life taking hold of the world to transfigure it. Therefore the question is not one of opposition between a speculative and an active attitude but between a natural life, whether speculative or active, and a supernatural life, which may also be either. And with regard to action, the opposition will be between a purely human, natural activity, and a supernatural activity, with the Holy Spirit as its source.

Now the man whom the Holy Ghost takes hold of to be His instrument in carrying out the works that will divinise the world is the prophet in the Old Testament, the apostle in the New. We get back here to the great truth underlying all our thought: there is always a sacred history going on, accomplished by the Holy Spirit, whereby all spiritual creation is divinised. This is a work of God's quite beyond man's mind to conceive. And the Holy Spirit carries it out by means of the human instruments He chooses. If they are to be of any use, the Holy Spirit must empty them entirely of self, take from them their own sight which is short and narrow, that they may enter fully into His views which are large and merciful. He must take from them their own wills, which are selfish and carnal, and reclothe them in wholly spiritual and disinterested dispositions. It is a whole mystery of death and resurrection, of overthrow and transformation, by which the Holy Spirit, who is a consuming fire, destroys the old man to make the apostle. By this divine action He moulds men utterly abandoned to Himself, drawn away from the world of seen history to live wholly in the world of sacred history whose witnesses and agents they are, to live in it, to live it.

Now we must try and get at the kind of spirituality this involves. It is clear that the purification of an apostle must be first a purification of his carnal and human outlook, of what Saint Paul calls "the thoughts of the flesh". These are the thoughts of our natural intellect, whereas God's outlook would be the outlook of faith. The apostle must be stripped of his natural way of viewing things so as to see Christ in everything. But it is most important that we should see exactly what this means. In

Saint John of the Cross we find a way of purification and holiness through the dark night of the senses and of the understanding which goes either to destroy or to overcome the natural action of the intellect, so that the soul may penetrate beyond any possible image, by faith alone, into the darkness of God. The purification of an apostle is not the least like this. His vocation is not to seek God *apart from* created things but *in* created things, God present to them by His transforming action. Jerome Nadal expressed this very forcefully in connection with Ignatian mysticism, which might be considered an apostolic and prophetic form of mysticism. "I shall never forget the grace he had, in all circumstances, undertakings and human contacts, of *feeling* God's presence and a longing for spiritual things, of being *a contemplative in the midst of action*, which he called: looking for God in everything."[1] The apostle must, it is quite true, live among created things. His problem is to turn these things from being an obstacle between himself and God into a means of union with God. One might express the whole of apostolic spirituality as a journey from one of these poles to the other. When the apostle sees all creatures as a sign of God's presence, and a means to union with Him, then this spirituality will have attained its object.

It becomes clear at once that abnegation in this sense deals not with things themselves, but with our use of them. What must be done away with is all spirit of selfishness, all obstinacy of mind, and their place must be filled by a true spiritual view of things. It is true that to carnal man what faith sees is sheer darkness, but here the stress is rather on how disconcerting God's plan is to our natural reason than how it transcends images. The apostle's faith is the faith Abraham had when God promised that

[1] *Epist.*, vol. iv, 651.

his seed should outnumber the stars in the sky, although his wife was barren; he believed in this Word despite all his experience told him, and did what God wanted. To be an apostle means to be called upon to undertake works which human reason sees as impossible, with only the light or faith for support. Intellect must reject all that earthly wisdom shows as certain, and lean entirely on what God says. That is what makes faith heroic. "In the promise also of God he staggered not by distrust; but was strengthened in faith, giving glory to God; most fully knowing that whatsoever he has promised he is able also to perform" (Rom. iv. 20–1).

The intellect is purified so as to take on the eyes of faith, and the will is correspondingly purified in a way that is essential to apostolic spirituality. Here again it is not so much a matter of having a dark night of all desires, but of a fundamental stripping away of self whereby one's own will is broken down, so that the soul wants only what God wants, and attaching itself to Him in love, actually prefers His will in all things. This again is a most deep and difficult purification. The soul must get rid of its own will and put in its place God's will. This means total abnegation. And this must be the light in which we see obedience. Obedience is the chief and essential means to that death of self-will which enables us to put on the will of God. It is essentially a way of union. We can only understand it if we give it this mystical dimension. The best writing on this subject is by Saint Alphonsus Rodriguez, who shows how obedience unites us directly with God's will working out our salvation: "God taught him an even more perfect obedience than the obedience of faith, which is believing what one cannot see. This more perfect obedience consists in doing what one sees and knows that God has ordered one to do, because He has ordered it." That is why it is one of the great mysteries of apostolic holiness: "All perfect virtues are a great mystery in the soul where God implants them, a mystery which can only be grasped by the perfect, to whom God has made it known. This mystery is a mystery of charity. By charity a soul can perform acts noble and heroic in the sight of God, acts not fully understood by those who see them; they sometimes appear to be imprudence or even madness, because the mystery of them is not understood." This is indeed in the realm of mystery, God's hidden plan which carnal man cannot get at, by which He carries out His great works in the world through the power of the Spirit. This is the mystery which obedience makes us begin to understand. And the apostle must be obedient if he is to be fully an instrument of God's ways.

This double purification of mind and will leads towards the transforming union. It is not simply a question of the soul's being conformed to God's way of thinking and acting. But, in proportion as the soul becomes emptied of itself and possessed by the Holy Ghost, it, too, Saint Paul tells us, will have a sort of obscure awareness, which is the mystical experience that belongs to the apostolic life. The very works the apostle does he seems no longer to feel as his own, he sees through to something beyond them, savours their spiritual meaning. Remember what Nadal said about Saint Ignatius' insisting that the presence of God felt in the exercise of the apostolic life was a fact of experience: "The grace he had in all circumstances . . . of *feeling* God's presence and the savour for spiritual things, of being a *contemplative in the midst of action*". Nadal also speaks elsewhere of Saint Ignatius wishing that his disciples "might feel no less *devotion* in doing any work of charity and obedience than they did during meditation itself."[1]

[1] *Ep. et Inst.*, iii, p. 500.

And Nadal himself gives an incomparable formula for apostolic mystical life: "The work of the Holy Ghost is to give us the life of the Spirit which is higher than the active or even the contemplative life by itself; in this life we do not merely live a spiritual and contemplative life, but we teach others, and show them the spiritual meaning of life itself." And elsewhere: "Never bring your mind to rest on any created thing without making it a means to see through it to God Himself, and Christ will give it its inner meaning."

The Holy Spirit gives everything an inner, a spiritual meaning, which is there for us to savour. The apostle is one who has got through to this inner meaning and communicates it to others.[1] The fire of the Spirit, kindled in him, tends to spread. It is the presence of the Holy Ghost Himself in the world trying to set everything on fire, taking possession of all who will let Him. It is the life of the Spirit flowing down in a great stream upon Christ, given on by Him at Pentecost to the Apostles, which flows through history—which makes history, one might say—and in which the apostle is so completely immersed that he realises that it is no longer he who acts, but the active presence of the Spirit which fills him, takes him out of himself and transforms him. The same thing that the might of the Spirit is working upon the whole world is also happening within each soul. This same reality is what the apostle sees in his heart of hearts and gazes at in an ecstasy of wonder. It is not merely a personal and subjective spirituality. The Holy Spirit takes possession of his very heart, and at the same time shows him His great works throughout history, past, present and future.[2]

[1] Nadal, *Journal Spiritual, Dieu Vivant*, v.
[2] "One seems to see God manifesting His power throughout the world", Nadal, *ibid.*

He dazzles him in adoration of the great works of the Old Testament, He overwhelms him in adoration of the Incarnation and the Resurrection, He unfolds before Him the great things far beyond human vision that He is to do in the ages of the Church, conversions, sanctifications, missions; He shows him the goal to which all things tend the glorious second coming of Christ which fills his soul with longing. And, lifted out of himself by measureless admiration, in a prophetic ecstasy, he can only cry as Mary did at the supreme moment when the Word was made flesh: *Magnificat anima mea Dominum*: "He that is mighty hath done great things. . . ."